Happiness:

the scientific path to achieving well-being

Vincenzo Berghella

Copyright Page

ISBN No: 978-0-578-13626-4

From the same author: (see also www.lulu.com)

- **Obstetric Evidence Based Guidelines.** Informa Healthcare, London, UK, and New York, USA (2007) [English]
- **Maternal Fetal Evidence Based Guidelines.** Informa Healthcare, London, UK, and New York, USA (2007) [English]
- **Laughter, the best medicine. Jokes for everyone.** (2007) [English]
- **Ridere, la migliore medicina. Barzellette per bambini.** (2007) [Italiano]
- **My favorite quotes.** (2009) [English]
- **In medio stat virtus – Citazioni d'autore.** (2009) [Italiano]
- **Quello che di voi vive in me.** (2009) [Italiano]
- **Dall'altra parte dell'oceano**. (2010) [Italiano]

[Translated in: **On the other side of the ocean**. (2013) [English]

- **Preterm Birth: Prevention and Management.** Wiley-Blackwell. Oxford, United Kingdom. (2010) [English]
- **From father to son.** (2010) [English]
- **Sollazzi.** (2010) [Italiano]

- **The land of religions.** (2011) [English] [Translated in: **La terra delle religioni.** (2013) [Italiano]
- **Giramondo.** (2011) [Italiano]
- **Obstetric Evidence Based Guidelines.** Informa Healthcare, London, UK, and New York, USA (2012; Second Edition) [English]
- **Maternal Fetal Evidence Based Guidelines.** Informa Healthcare, London, UK, and New York, USA (2012; Second Edition) [English]
- **Trip to London.** (2012) [English]
- **Il primo amore non si scorda mai**. (2012) [Italiano]
- **Maldives.** (2013) [English]
- **Russia.** (2013) [English]

Index

"Happiness is not something that happens to people, but something they make happen."

Mikaly Csikszentmihalyi

Introduction

"Happiness is the meaning and the purpose of life, the whole aim and end of human existence."[1]

Aristotle

One of the happiest moments of my life occurred on October 18, 2012. While we were talking on the phone, my father told me that I've done better in life than he did. He recognized my strengths, my strong social relationships at home and at work, the fact that I had pursued my personal dreams and made them come true, while helping others around me to have a better life.

The majority of people around the world, consistently in every nation, state that one of their most important, if not the most important, goals in life, is being happy.[2,3] Happiness represents the ultimate aim in life and the truest measure of well-being.[4] People seek happiness for themselves, and even more, if they have them, for their children. For all of you who want to be unhappy in life, this is a good time to switch books.

As the Nobel Prize-winning scientist Daniel Kahneman said, people are often surprisingly bad judges of what will make them happy.[5] For example, they move to places with warmer weather, unaware that climate does not influence happiness much. They buy a new fancy car thinking their mood will improve, only to get used to it in a few weeks and soon cease to gain any satisfaction from the expense.

There is a lot of research on what activities are most effective at making us happy. So, I want to approach happiness from a scientific point of view. While this is not a scientific book, i.e. a boring book, its basis is the scientific data, the evidence, behind what makes us happy. I am a physician myself, and I've learned that the scientific approach which is used in medicine, can be applied to everyday life, to decide the best course of action for just about everything.

There are several scientific journals devoted to publishing exclusively scholarly research on happiness, which include, among others, The Journal of Happiness Studies, The Journal of Happiness and Well-Being, The International Journal of Happiness and Development, and The Journal of Positive Psychology.

I also reviewed studies from some of the best scientific journals in the world, such as The Lancet. I focused especially on randomized studies, which provide the most reliable scientific data. Moreover, I researched this topic by reading several relatively recent scholarly books on happiness,[6,7,8,9,10,11] and international scientific reports.[12]

The aim of this book is to review the evidence to successfully pursue happiness, presenting the issues like an easy cook book, a clear guide, to follow closely to achieve happiness. It is possible to train the mind just as the body. It is possible to train the mind to be happy. It just takes two actions. First, recognizing what makes us happy. Second, practicing repeatedly the exercises and daily voluntary acts which make us happy.

Not everyone defines happiness the same way. And not everyone achieves happiness the same way. There is probably no absolute single meaning for happiness: happiness is relative to the person experiencing it. Well-being, which many use synonymously with happiness, is somewhat subjective, and we all achieve it a bit differently. Most truly, the best judge of how happy you are is you.[13]

So you'll have to pick and choose from this long list of proven opportunities. The right to pursue happiness does not mean each path to it is similar. It will depend on your unique values, interests, and needs. In fact, a state which mandates community service or going to church may be counterproductive, as each of us is different and must find what works best for herself or himself.[14]

But, as you'll see reading this book, science has discovered several facts which we can all apply to our lives to improve our well-being. As you have probably noticed in life, and as has been said by noted happiness researchers, "happy people are all alike."[15]

I won't discuss, on purpose, about depression and negative moods and emotions, as those have been studied and reported so many times in the past. I will review the scientific evidence for positive mood, instead. Of course, all the positive benefits of happiness can be seen also, looking at the other side of the coin, in light of the harms of unhappiness, depression, and anxiety, but the trick is to look at the glass half full, to generate positive emotions. Like in medicine, for overall well-being the best approach is to work on prevention, not on treatment of disease.

Brief history of the pursuit of happiness

"The constitution only guarantees the American people the right to pursue happiness. You have to catch it yourself."

Benjamin Franklin

There are several philosophical, religious, ethical, and political roots from which today's more scientific studies in happiness stem. It is worthwhile to review a selected list of these origins of happiness, to appreciate that much of what we know today has old foundations, but also realize that current developments have not only confirmed but vastly expanded on ancient wisdom.

The Greek philosopher Aristotle is still one of the most quoted authors on happiness. In the *Nicomachean Ethics*, written in 350 BCE, he stated that happiness is the only thing that humans desire for its own sake, unlike riches, honor, health or friendship. He observed that men sought riches, or honor, or health, not only for their own sake but also in order to be happy, which meant being well, doing well.

Eudaimonia (Greek: εὐδαιμονία) is a classical Greek word commonly translated as 'happiness.' Etymologically, it consists of the word "eu" ("good" or "well-being") and "daimōn" ("spirit" or "minor deity," used by extension to mean one's lot or fortune). For Aristotle, Eudaimonia is an activity rather than an emotion or a state.

Happiness is characteristic of a good life, that is, a life in which a person fulfills human nature in an excellent way. People have a set of purposes which are typically human: these belong to our nature. The happy person is virtuous, meaning she has outstanding abilities and emotional tendencies which allow her to fulfill our common human ends. For Aristotle, then, happiness is "the virtuous activity of the soul in accordance with reason." Happiness is the practice of virtue. After him, practically all philosophers and religious thinkers have defined happiness in terms of living a good life, or flourishing, rather than simply as an emotion.

Also about 2300 years ago, the Chinese Confucian thinker Mencius was convinced that the mind played a mediating role between the "lesser self" (the physiological self) and the "greater self" (the moral self), and that getting the priorities right between these two would lead to sagehood. He argued that if we did not feel satisfaction or pleasure in nourishing one's "vital force" with "righteous deeds," that force would shrivel up.[16] More specifically, he mentioned the experience of intoxicating joy if one celebrates the practice of the great virtues.[17]

Happiness forms a central theme in Buddhist teachings. For ultimate freedom from suffering, the Noble Eightfold Path leads its practitioner to Nirvana, a state of everlasting peace. Ultimate happiness is only achieved by overcoming craving in all forms. Other forms of happiness, such as maintaining good friendships, are also recognized as worthy goals. Buddhism also encourages the generation of loving kindness and compassion, the desire for the happiness and welfare of all beings.[18]

In Catholicism, the ultimate end of human existence consists in 'felicity' (Latin equivalent to the Greek *eudaimonia*), or "blessed happiness," described by the 13th-century philosopher-theologian Thomas Aquinas as the pursuit of good causes for acts, such as habits according to virtue.[19]

The Muslim Sufi thinker Al-Ghazali (1058–1111) wrote the Alchemy of Happiness, a manual of spiritual instruction throughout the Muslim world and widely practiced today. The Hindu thinker Patanjali, author of the Yoga Sutras, wrote quite exhaustively on the psychological and ontological roots of bliss.[20]

Many ethicists have made arguments for how humans should behave, either individually or collectively, based on the resulting happiness of such behavior. Utilitarians, such as John Stuart Mill and Jeremy Bentham, advocated the greatest happiness principle as a guide for ethical behavior.

In politics, the French Constitution, on June 24th, 1793, stated "*Le but de la societe' est le bonheur commun.*" It means, 'The goal of society is general happiness.'[21] This was one of the first political statements regarding happiness, and was based on the work of several theorists, including Cesare Beccaria, Claude-Adrien Helvetius, and Francis Hutcheson, among others.[22]

Thomas Jefferson, later a famous US President, added 'the pursuit of happiness' to the Declaration of Independence: "We hold these truths to be self-evident, that all men are created equal, that they are endowed by their Creator with certain unalienable rights, that among these are Life, Liberty and the pursuit of Happiness."

But, as we'll see in detail in this book, and was eminently said by Jefferson's contemporary Benjamin Franklin, when they were both living in my home town, Philadelphia, "The constitution only guarantees the American people the right to pursue happiness. You have to catch it yourself." In fact, Sonja Lyubomirsky, a leading scientific researcher of happiness, prefers to talk about the 'creation or construction of happiness,' instead of just the 'pursuit of happiness.'[23] Let's start digging first into what happiness is, so we can then generate it.

Definition of happiness

"Happiness is feeling that your life is going well"

Sissela Bok

My favorite definition of happiness is, "Happiness is the joy we feel striving after our potential."[24] Happiness is a mental state of well-being characterized by positive emotions ranging from contentment to intense joy.[25] The ten most common positive emotions have been said to be joy, gratitude, serenity, interests, hope, pride, amusement, inspiration, awe, and love.[26] Happiness refers to the experience of joy, contentment, or positive well-being, combined with a sense that one's life is good, meaningful, and worthwhile.[27] Happiness implies a positive mood in the present and a positive outlook for the future.

Many, including Aristotle, Freud, and others, have also tried to define happiness. In fact, a variety of biological, psychological, religious, and philosophical approaches have striven to define happiness and identify its sources. Some have argued that we do not even need a definition of happiness, because we know subjectively if we are happy or not. Happiness is a by-product that comes as a result of doing other things, and so cannot be a goal in itself.

But, as we'll see in this book, there is actually a lot of scientific data about what makes us happy, and what does not, at least in general. In the scientific literature, 'well-being' (or 'subjective' well-being) is often used interchangeably with 'happiness,' and I will also do so in this book. Still others have also used 'satisfaction with life', 'positive emotions,' and 'positivity' as synonyms with happiness.

The science of 'Positive psychology' strives to apply the scientific method to answer questions about what "happiness" is, and how we might attain it. Happiness comes from within an individual, and depends less on outside circumstances than on the individual internal perceptions and related emotions. That is why scientists talk about 'Synthetic happiness.' We synthesize happiness, within ourselves; we do not find happiness.

As everyone is different inside, everyone has a bit of a personal definition of happiness. Happiness therefore can mean many things to many people. Part of the challenge of the science of happiness is to identify all the various components of happiness, those proven to help us achieve well-being, and then it is up to each of us to find the particular activities which makes us personally happy.

Happiness can be measured

Happiness, even if clearly a subjective issue, can be measured, in several ways. Happiness can be measured objectively. The Organization for Economic Cooperation and Development (OECD) has published Guidelines on Measuring Subjective Well-being, as reported in the World Happiness Report 2013.[28] These are quite extensive, rigorous, and evidence-based, meaning based on well-designed scientific studies.

Three elements relate to the definition of subjective well-being: 1. *Life evaluation* – a reflective assessment on a person's life or some specific aspect of it; 2. *Eudaimonia* – a sense of meaning and purpose in life, or good psychological functioning; and 3. *Affect* – a person's feelings or emotional states, typically measured with reference to a particular point in time.

A distinction should then be made from current emotion ("Are you happy right now?"), versus overall evaluation ("Are you happy in general with your life?"). *Current emotion* often has to do with pleasure, such as licking a candy, receiving a caress, and other often physical enjoyments. This is called the 'affective' measure of happiness. Measures of *positive emotion* (or positive affect) are often asked about the day preceding the survey.

Overall *life evaluation* of happiness has to do more with gratifications, and is what almost all good happiness surveys test for, as reported by the World Happiness Report.[29] They evaluate happiness with life as a whole. Overall satisfaction with life is called the 'evaluative' measure of happiness.

The OECD primary measure of subjective well-being is the life evaluation question, "Overall, how satisfied are you with life as a whole these days?" The second core question relates to eudaimonia, "Overall, to what extent do you feel the things you do in your life are worthwhile?"

The last three of the five core measures of subjective well-being have to do with affect, and ask about how a person felt yesterday, "How about happy?" "How about worried?" "How about depressed?" Three leading life evaluations are the Catril ladder of life,[30] life satisfaction,[31] and happiness with life as a whole.[32] Another popular happiness test is the Subjective Happiness Scale.[33]

As we embark in looking at the activities which science has proven most associated with happiness, we must first be aware how reliable these data are. Some are based on the experimental method, which is the best. People get randomized to either one or another activity, and then compared for levels of happiness. For example, the fact that we are happier giving than receiving has some of this science – the best – behind it.[34]

Other issues cannot be studied easily this way, for example happiness in relation to salary, or religion. In these cases, usually two groups of people which differ in the factor (e.g. very religious, versus atheist) are compared, either looking at what they have done in the past (retrospective), or studying them for a certain period going forward from now (prospective).

In general, prospective data are more reliable than retrospective. Also, factors which may influence the outcome (e.g. how many married versus single persons there are while studying the influence of salary) should be controlled for, i.e. equal in the groups. Of course, in general, the larger is the study, the better is the science.

Another important factor in studying happiness is how the questions are asked. For example, people tend to be happier thinking about the past, compared to when they are asked suddenly how happy they are at that very exact moment. In retrospect, people may attach more positive values even to trying times, such as surviving through a difficult task in the past.

Also, the sequence of questions can significantly alter how respondents answer. What happened just before the question can also alter the response. Happiness on September 12, 2001 was certainly less than on September 10, 2001, no matter the person or moment during those two days. In fact, culture can alter happiness answers, as some countries or some groups of people may not feel comfortable seeming happy compared to others.[35]

I could go on and on explaining these factors, but feel confident that at least I just made you aware that not all scientific data are equal. On the other hand, much of scientific research on happiness is not only reliable, but also reproducible. One's evaluation of her subjective well-being correlates with the opinions of friends and relatives about how happy the person really is.[36] Moreover, people who describe themselves as happy smile more often and more genuinely than less content controls.[37] As we'll see later, people who self-report being happy have a long list of objective benefits, including better jobs, marriages, and health, leading even to longer lives.[38]

To those who still argue that some of these scientifically-proven means to assess levels of happiness are still too linked to people's perceptions, one should be reminded of other facts. First, it is usually people's own perceptions of the state of their persona and of those around them, including the world as a whole, which drive individual behavior, rather than 'measurements of the facts.'[39] Second, measurements of *human development* are closely correlated with measurements of life satisfaction.

Measures of human development (which go in the Human Development Index [HDI]) are life expectancy at birth; years of schooling; gross national income per capita; job satisfaction; freedom of choice; inequality; trust in government; perceptions of safety; and economic conditions. These can be measured even more objectively, and are very closely correlated, individually and as a whole (in the HDI), with life satisfaction and happiness.[40] Goals of human development overlap considerably with determinants of happiness.

I'm happy to report that the world has become a slightly happier and more generous place over the past five years, with continuous progress towards equality, better lives, and social support.[41]

What determines happiness?

"God, grant me the serenity to accept the things I cannot change, the courage to change the things I can, and the wisdom to know the difference."

Reinhold Niebuhr

What determines your happiness? Lots of scientific work, in particular by Sonja Lyubomirsky,[42] has shown that happiness depends on three main factors, as shown in this figure:

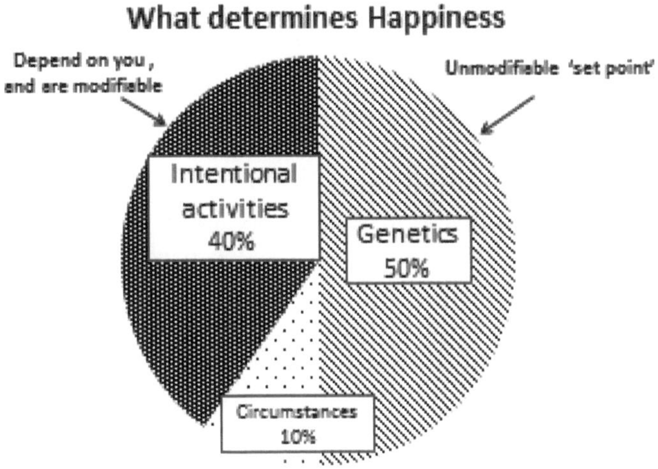

Happiness depends on nature (genetics), on what we decide to do (intentional activities), and on external factors which happen to us (circumstances).

Genetics

Somewhat sadly, 50% of our happiness level is set at conception, when your mother's egg meets your father's spermatozoon. Half of happiness depends on the specific 'happiness' genes you were passed on from your parents. Just as some people have long bones or are better predisposed, for example, at high jump, other people won the cortical lottery and excel at being happy. A good portion of the story of someone's life is written at birth, even at conception; some of the seeds of happiness are planted in the genes.

This evidence comes in significant part from twin studies. Research on identical and fraternal twins suggests that each of us is born with a particular happiness set point.[43] In fact, in identical twins, sharing the exact same DNA, the levels of happiness are very similar even if major facts and events in their lives were different. Marriage accounts for less than 1% difference, and income for less than 2% difference.[44]

For fraternal twins instead, who have the same DNA differences that any other brother and sister, happiness levels vary greatly despite 50% of similar DNA.

Happiness genes, and especially 'depression genes' (for example the 5-HTTLPR gene,[45] which codes for the serotonin transporter promoter), are constantly being discovered. Interestingly, though, these genes make us vulnerable, but they do not necessarily cause the condition they are associated with. People with the 'bad' allele for the 5-HTTLPR gene, do not become depressed if they have a supportive family and positive life experiences.[46]

Happy people seem to have more activity in the left prefrontal cortex than in the right.[47] This may be our brain happiness center, according to electroencephalographic functional studies of our emotions.[48] This baseline 'set point' level does not change, but we can improve it, or lower it, mostly based on our own chosen activities.

Interestingly, this concept is similar to our genetically-predisposed set point for weight.[49] I seem to have a tendency for being at the top normal of weight range, just as my dad. My wife and older son seem to be blessed to be genetically determined to be skinny, no matter how much they eat.

So, just as we can beat our set point for weight, or for cholesterol, we can improve our set point for happiness. The worst people can do is believe they cannot change. People who have opinions such as 'I'm wired to be unhappy,' 'women are not good at math,' 'he was born a criminal,' 'I just cannot do this,' have to shed these myths, because that's what they are, non-truths.

Brain change is possible depending on how you live your life. Taxi drivers have larger hippocampi, the brain structure devoted to spacial memory, than average people. Our thoughts, activities, and behaviors, can change our brain. Let's see how.

Intentional activities

Fortunately, and most importantly, 40% of our level of happiness is determined by the activities we choose. These are things we consciously select to do, like spending time with our loved ones, meditation, or jogging, which have a greater promise for increasing our happiness than other activities.

So we can control, and determine ourselves, by our choices, a significant part of how happy we can be. Intentional activities can also be called voluntary activities. I do prefer the term intentional, as it emphasizes that we want to do them. It is not just that we could do them if we wanted to.

Happiness, as introduced earlier, is inside us, not outside. It is not something we need to go looking somewhere for, and find. We make our own happiness, with our own actions, and therefore it is a state of mind, a way of perceiving and approaching ourselves and the world in which we live.[50]

Happiness is not determined much by an individual's material conditions, such as money, or even health, but mostly by the individual's moral character. Later chapters are devoted to review the activities we can chose to proactively increase our happiness. In brief summary, these include intrinsic goals, such as relationship with others, doing what you like to do, having aims which have great personal meaning, dedication, and recognition.

External circumstances

Only about 10% of the variance in our happiness level depends on differences in life conditions. These are usually external elements. They include factors we cannot change, like race, gender, and age. And they also include issues we can alter somewhat, like marital status, where we live (geographic, house, bed, etc), occupation, income, health status, how beautiful (or not!), what car we drive, and how rich we are.[51,52] As these conditions tend to be long lasting, we get used to them, resulting in little influence on our overall happiness.

So, overall, up to 50% of our happiness, adding the 40% of intentional activities to the 10% of circumstances, is for the vast part under our own control. Intentional activities and circumstances are related to the fact that happiness, in certain ways, depends on a set of needs.

Abraham Maslow listed these needs in order of priority, resulting in his famous pyramid:[53]

People must have some basics before being able to feel happiness. First, humans must have physiological essentials such as food, water, shelter, warmth, sleep, as the core necessities of life. Then, they must feel safe and secure. Without these first two basic sets of needs at the base of the pyramid, no happiness can be built. People without safety, food, and shelter, report being very unhappy. Some money for medical care, nutrition, and even basic simple toys for children create a lot more happiness compared to those lacking these simple essentials.[54,55]

Only once these fundamentals are present, the next three levels can be built on. As we'll see confirmed by a lot more scientific data, social relationships and a sense of belonging, achieving mastery and recognition in work we love to do as if we are playing, and pursuing goals which are meaning for ourselves in making a better world, bring us to the top of the pyramid.

So, while short term we may enjoy pleasures, medium term well-being includes achievement of goals and satisfactions. Those who practice happiness skills (even without knowing they do) can reach the long term ultimate goals of finding the reason for their life, and of fulfilling their potential.

Your attitude

"There is nothing either good or bad, but thinking makes it so."

William Shakespeare[56]

There is a story, as told by my friend and colleague Mike Foley, which gives the true meaning of what the right attitude a human should have going through life.[57]

A blind man goes to visit a friend. At the end of the visit, just before saying goodbye and heading back through the usual path to go home, the blind man asks his friend for a candle, as it is now dark outside. The friend is puzzled, and asks, "Why do you need a candle, as you are blind, and you also know the path by heart as you have walked it hundreds of times?"

The blind man says, "I do not need the candle for myself. I need the candle so that others can see me, and so to protect them from bumping into me." So the friend gives a lighted candle to the blind man, who leaves and starts walking down his usual path home.

After about 15 minutes, BOOM, someone hits the blind man, and he falls to the soil. This is the whole story. What is its meaning?

The lighted candle represents our passions, our interests, our reciprocity, our sociability. The meaning of the story is that if we ourselves do not carry a light while going along our path, we go through life without ever being noticed. Without ever making a difference. We are the ones in charge of our life, and we need to have the candle lighted, both for our and for others' benefit. Carry a bright candle, make a difference.

Happiness is "a way of interpreting the world, since while it is difficult to change the world [but you should try], it is always possible to change the way you look at it."[58] You need to have the willingness to first learn what has been proven to make people happy, by having an open and attentive mind to the scientific evidence we review. Then, you have to have the strength of character and dedication to implement in your life the actions proven to make you happier.

There is evidence suggesting that people can improve their happiness. Everyone can benefit, to varying degrees, from the various habits and practices identified by positive psychology. In adulthood, what most correlates with happiness is optimism, extroversion, a feeling that you have control over your life, and self-esteem. These, if not innate, can be vastly improved.

Feelings of joy, delight, contentment, serenity, curiosity, interest, vitality, enthusiasm, vigor, thrill, pride: these are the positive emotions that make happy people who they are, and are the hallmark of happiness in another study.[59] Positive emotions usually cause more happy moments, in a positive feedback cycle.

For example, aerobic exercise invigorates you, so that then you are more creative, and therefore you come up with a new idea, which then improves your relationship with a loved one, which then makes you more productive at work, leading eventually to a better sense of personal well-being.

So positive emotions trigger positive activities, and also make us look at things in a more positive way, leading us to 'experience' life more positively. Happy moods then lead people to be more likeable, happier, friendlier, and more helpful. Positive emotions help achieve our goals. One would want to be happy not just for the feeling of it, but because it makes us more successful.

The next chapter explores the main intentional activities which make us happy.

The six intentional activities which create happiness

"Happiness consists in activity. It is a running stream, not a stagnant pool."

John Mason Good

There are various activities which have been best correlated with happiness. The six activities which we can intentionally chose to perform, making them habits of our daily life, and which have been most strongly scientifically correlated with increases in happiness, are social relationships, doing what you like to do, having goals, finding a greater meaning, working hard, and recognition. Psychologist Martin Seligman, with his Positive Psychology research, is the one who has most contributed to developing this list.[60]

It is important to distinguish between the activities which give, in general, longer-lasting happiness, as for example relationships, engagement, meaning, and accomplishments, and those which, in general, give shorter bursts of happiness, such as pleasures.

Social relationships

"To find a friend is to find a treasure"

Siracides 6, 14-15

The first and most important key to happiness is having strong social relationships. Human relationships and connections of all kinds contribute more to happiness than anything else.[61] Social ties are an extremely reliable indicator of happiness. Most people who have good friends are happier to begin with. Also, most individuals tend to be happier when they are with other people than when they are alone.

In a famous study, 268 Harvard College students were followed for 40 years to identify life circumstances and personal characteristics associated with happiness. The findings were: 'Love – full stop.' Relationships with other people - partner, family, friends, colleagues - matter more than anything else in the world.[62] In another study, the characteristic of the happiest 10% of us was the strength of our social relationship.[63]

There are many social relationships which boost happiness. These include spending time with your partner, or a close friend, but also belonging to a club where you have good friends.

The most important choice in your life will be who you want to relate with the most, at home, on vacation, during weekends, at night. This is your co-pilot, your life companion. This is the person you rely on, you care for, you trust, you donate to the most. If passionate love is fire, this compassionate love, which takes years to solidify, can be compared to vines intertwining as they grow, given the positive social interaction.[64]

Having a few best friends is also associated with happiness. These are the people to whom we can share our innermost secrets, and doubts. These are those who we know won't judge us, but will instead help us in times of trouble, or just answer our most difficult questions.

Finding a good mentor can also be seen as a social relationship which creates well-being. As Frank Bucaro said, "Don't wait for someone to take you under their wing. Find a good wing and climb up underneath it." Whenever you meet someone you admire and you want to be like, try to spend a bit more time with them, to know them. Sir Isaac Newton said, "It is only by standing on the shoulders of giants, that I've been able to see further." It's true.

Social groups of almost any kind boost happiness. For example, attending monthly club meetings or volunteering once a month is associated with the same change in well-being as a doubling of income.[65]

Group social support can help in many other ways, including

remarkable improvements in health. Breast cancer support group members had twice the life expectancy of non-members.[66] In a study of people trying to lose weight, those who did it together with three acquaintances, friends, or family members had a 66% success rate (lost more weight, kept it off, for longer) at 6 months, compared to only 24% for those who went about it alone.[67]

Lots of things that have to do with socializing (e.g. seeing friends, having a lovable family, having sex) are very important, in fact key, for happiness. So spend money on activities, not on material things. Have dinner with friends. Enjoy movies with loved ones. Happiness is relatively cheap. Actually, most of happiness is free.

Knowing who your neighbors are, and especially being friendly with your neighbor, is one of the keys to happiness. This can be seen anywhere, including in less affluent communities, anywhere in the world, where the sense of community, of mutual help, of being able to help the person next to us creates a profound sense of well-being. Often, in your neighborhood you'll find people similar to you, in terms of values and interests. You should invite them over for a small get together, and keep the ones you are closest to intellectually in frequent contact with you. You should treat them as they were part of your extended family.

Feel part of a team. Once you feel connected to some group larger than yourself – family, team, class, school, town, group of friends, the high-risk pregnancy specialists of the world – you do not want to harm that group by doing wrong, or by not giving your best. You will naturally want to do your part to remain a respected and valued member of the group. It feels better to win as part of a team, a bigger effort, than just for yourself. So connectedness leads to moral behavior, because you embrace the values of your group. You feel connected to a mission in life.

Who is your team? My team started with my mother, my father, my sister Anna, my brother Michele. It then wonderfully expanded to my wife Paola, and our children Andrea and Pietro. Now it includes also my in-laws, my nieces and nephews, my closest friends, my dearest colleagues, my patients. I want to win for them.

Be part of a team you like, trust, interact well with, admire. After students with low grade-point averages start to room with higher-scoring students, their grade-point averages increase.[68] One happy player can improve the mood of the whole team; and the happier the team is, the better they play.[69]

When interviewed at retirement, successful professionals said that what most motivated them at work was the stimulus from their colleagues, the work friendships, and in general the people they worked with.[70] The greatest predictor of a team's success is how team members feel about each other.[71] The more members socialize and interact face-to-face, the better are the results of their work.[72]

So 'socialize' at work, whether you are in a leadership situation, or in a rank-and-file position. Listen to others' problems, introduce employees to each other, express interest, listen to others, express gratitude, collaborate, help, 'manage by walking around,' a concept popularized by Tom Peters in the 1980's.

Perhaps the most important social relationship at work is with your boss. Employees with strong positive bonds with their manager bring in more money, and stay with the company longer.[73] Employees with difficult rapport with their boss have higher blood pressure, and a 30% higher chance of coronary artery disease.[74]

There is science that says that the best groups are made of between about 4 and 8 people. And that the best conversations, if both persons are willing to listen and talk positively, are one-on-one. I like to talk with my parents one at a time, if possible.

A key to a good social life is being able to communicate effectively. A good place to look for wisdom is in the minds of people with different skills than you, and even in your opponents. The best conversations are those in which your attention is so focused that you forget what time it is, and you forget what else is going on around you.

The key is to focus on what the other person is saying. The goals are to give space to the other face-to-face partner, to deeply understand their point of view, to learn as much as possible about the speaker's inner feelings and thoughts. That is why we have two ears, and only one mouth: listen more than you speak.

Deep social ties come from exposing ourselves candidly to our peers. This means often being vulnerable, as we share our fears, weaknesses, faults. Open people gain trust from others by recognizing, and then sharing their vulnerabilities. Showing your human side inevitably gains the other person's trust.[75] Tell people what you always wanted to tell them. That is why I have written so many personal books, and I share so many intimate stories with the people I love.

As we'll see in more detail later, recognition is a key to happiness. But recognition which comes from our social group is far more important than recognition which comes from the public. If I analyze my emotions carefully, I have discovered that I care a lot more about a phrase of praise from my parents, than about an international award. A direct impact on my nephew from a book I wrote counts for me a lot more than selling 10,000 copies of that book. Achieving success in our own backyard, to the eyes of family members and closest friends, is the best way to flourish. If professional success comes at great costs to loved ones near us, that success is bitter sweet, and often will eventually lead to unhappiness.

Make sure you always treat people with respect. Make the other person feel more important than you are during the interaction. That is why people bow in martial arts as they meet, to show each other respect. Your peer must first know you care, before she cares what you know.[76]

When you connect with your peer, remember the concept of reciprocity. It is in giving love that we receive love. It is in giving that we receive. Treat everyone else like you would like to be treated. As the African civil right poet Maya Angelou said, "People may not remember exactly what you say, or what you have done, but they always remember how you made them feel." Make them feel you care.

How would you feel if, with an angry face, I yelled unpleasantly at you, "You are the best colleague I ever had!" And how would you feel (as acted by my friend Mike Foley) if I sat next to you, put my arm around you, looked you lovingly in the eyes, and with a calm and sweet voice I murmured, "Oh, dear, you just have no talent for anything." Form is everything. Attitude is everything. Be nice. Performing acts of kindness to others, as we would want to receive them, is associated with a significant increase in levels of happiness. The world lives on reciprocity.

There is scientific evidence that relationships change our hormones and physiology. Positive social connections increase our blood levels of oxytocin, a 'pleasure-inducing' hormone, reducing anxiety and improving concentration and focus, and lower levels of cortisol, the stress hormone.[77]

Having insufficient social connections can be as deadly as certain diseases. People with few social ties have two to three times more depression than people with strong social bonds.[78] Two of my medical school classmates died during the first two grueling years of heavy, continuous, isolated studying. One died of anorexia. The other falling from a window on the ninth floor. Please make sure you are always safe, seek support from others, and, loved ones, always be present if and when necessary. Parents and good friends should continue to give unconditional love and support.

Doing what you like to do

"I just went ahead doing what I liked to do"

Linus Pauling

The second key to happiness is doing what we like to do. Do you remember, as a child, when you spent hours playing your favorite game? Playing with cards, a board game, some sport, Legos? You forgot what time it was, where you were, you were oblivious to anything else going on around you. You were in a state of flow. Happiness occurs when as an adult one finds a kind of play that people are willing to pay him to do.

For me play is figuring out a difficult diagnosis, reviewing the literature to make sure I have the latest management algorithm and therapy, teaching students, residents, and fellows, who are as passionate as I am about making lives better, as well as writing medical science and non-fiction books.

Linus Pauling, the Nobel laureate for Chemistry in 1954 and for Peace in 1962, said, "I do not think I ever sat down and asked myself, now what am I going to do in life? I just went ahead doing what I liked to do." By doing what you are interested in doing, you usually play to your strengths, which is a well-proven key to personal and professional success.

When you are concentrated and immersed in a task you like, that's happiness, that status is flow. Examples for me are when I'm writing scientific papers. I concentrate during any free moments in the day about what to write next, how to analyze the data, what the results mean, how to organize the discussion, and what to really conclude based on the new scientific information we have gathered. Basically I keep on 'playing' for several days with whatever project I concentrate on, anticipating how much fun it is going to be when I can get back to work on that favorite project.

The more I find myself in this flow state of mind, the happier I am as a person. I am often in flow when I listen carefully to the history of a patient. I'm in flow when carefully operating during a cesarean delivery. I'm in flow right now, writing this book.

To reach a state of flow, the challenge inherent in the activity should match the skill of the person involved. You know you have high motivation when you do something because you truly believe that the experience (or its consequences) will ultimately be, for you, interesting, and stimulating, and enjoyable.

By challenging yourself, you will discover yourself. You'll discover virtues and strengths you never thought you had. You'll discover your limits. Two years ago, I was having a deep conversation with one of my good friends, Pierluigi. He was the other straight A's student in my class in high school. I was the 'scientist,' he was the 'philosopher.' I've always deeply admired his smart intellect, and his immense culture.

On a hill overlooking the Umbrian valley below Perugia, he told me, "You are lucky Vincenzo, as you know who you are. Life in the US has challenged you to discover your strengths, and use them to grow as a person. I do not know who I am. I never discovered if there is something I'm good at." It was a very sad moment. But, as always, he had revealed to me a profound truth.

Go to a school, join a work environment, where you will be exposed to as many different opportunities, facts, styles, mentors. Teachers and supervisors will start to notice your specific qualities, when you are having the most fun, and help you on the road to choosing your individual way of contributing to the happiness of human kind.

Medicine makes many happy because they will be doing things that stretch their skills. Medicine does this for me - and others - every day. The fact that it is challenging should be the fun. The prerequisite for happiness is to get fully involved in life, not partially involved.

I got exposed to all the many specialties of medicine in Medical School, and got to *play* a lot. One of my strongest memories is when I got to hold a beating heart. I rotated during my third year in cardiothoracic surgery, and they let me scrub in and participate in cardiac bypass surgery.

My job allows me to do what I do best. People work best when they are internally motivated, when they are allowed to pursue their intrinsic motives, doing it for the satisfaction they receive from good work. Unhappiness comes instead from being ordered around constantly or being motivated just by financial rewards.

Having goals

"An aim in life is the only fortune worth finding."

Robert Louis Stevenson

The third key to happiness is having goals to pursue. Having goals in and of itself is strongly associated with higher levels of happiness. There is no happiness without action.[79] Happiness is action!! Even for Aristotle, back over 2000 years ago, happiness was an activity, rather than an emotion or a state. Find something important to do, and that you are good at, and concentrate on it. People who strive for something personally significant are much happier than those who do not have strong dreams or aspirations.[80]

An Australian psychiatrist by the name of W. Beran Wolfe said it well: "If you observe a really happy man, you will find him building a boat, writing a symphony, educating his son, growing double dahlias in his garden, or looking for dinosaur eggs in the Gobi desert."[81] Find a happy person, and you will find a project.[82]

Devote your life to something meaningful for yourself. It does not matter as much as it has to do directly or indirectly with your work, or with making improvements to family, social, or spiritual lives. The process of working toward a goal, a challenging yet personally rewarding experience, is as important to well-being as its attainment.[83]

Having meaningful goals bolsters our self-esteem. It

stimulates us to feel confident, and efficacious. It adds structure and meaning to our lives. It leads us to develop responsibilities, and opportunities for mastering new skills. Aristotle said that to achieve *arete* (ἀρετή, happiness, excellence, virtue), we need to aim for *telos* (τέλος, a goal, purpose). He said that people are like archers, who need a clear target at which to aim.[84]

While goals should vary depending on the individual, there are some characteristics of these goals which make them most effective to achieve happiness. First, the goal should be personal. The goal should be intrinsic, self-developed, rewarding to the person pursuing it. It should not be forced on by outside pressure, such as a parent, a boss, a family member. We are more likely to be passionate about our own intrinsic goals, to pursue them actively, to work hard toward accomplishing them, and therefore eventually these are the goals we are most likely to be successful at achieving. Pursuing authentic goals is associated with higher levels of happiness, more health, and more success in completing the goal.[85] As an example, if you are an extrovert, you might enjoy most goals which involve interacting with people. Knowing which goal fits you best is an important skill, and necessitates self-awareness and emotional intelligence.[86] The ancient Greeks called "know thyself" (γνῶθι σεαυτόν) this capacity of introspection.

A second characteristic of good goals to pursue is making the aim a positive (e.g. I want to be healthy and feel good by exercising) rather than a negative one (e.g. I do not want to be fat). There is really a subtle difference here, as it may seem as this is the same goal. But chiefly pursuing avoidance goals, or conceptualizing our own goals as such, is associated with less happiness, more anxiety, distress, and less health, compared to pursuing 'approach' goals.[87]

A third characteristic of effective goals is that they should have value and meaning. One is more likely to persevere and achieve goals which have a larger purpose or long-term importance. More on this in the next section.

A fourth characteristic is that goals should help us experience ever new challenges, and involve us with new activities which match our increasing (or at times decreasing) expertise.

A fifth helpful characteristic of best goals to pursue is to make them harmonious, i.e. having goals which complement each other. Having at the same time the goals of spending more time with the kids, and helping them be better persons by being an example of the virtues we want to see in them, is such an example.

A sixth characteristic is that goals should be appropriate for age, i.e. at 49 the goal may be to finish a triathlon (I did it!), not to win it. Priorities change over time. We may list first our goals, and then decide which ones are most important to achieve now, or at least in the short term, and which ones may be most achievable later in life.

We may also decide at some point to give up on some goals. When I was thirty, I gave up on my goal of surfing, after I found that, even in my best shape, I could not master Hawaiian waves. You also need to have flexibility in your goal-pursuing. While it might be difficult to change the situation (called 'primary' control), it might be easier to change how one views the situation, i.e. to modify and realign your goal ('secondary' control).

It is helpful to write your goals down. What would you like to influence, because it matters most to you? How would you like to be seen by others? How would you like to be remembered? In addition, check the goals on your list from time to time, as they may change: some you achieve, some slightly change, or some you may not be interested in as much as before.

It is important to break down goals in feasible steps. Learning Spanish may first involve signing up for lessons, then buying software, then attending classes and doing homework, then perhaps even spending time in a country with native speakers. It might also be helpful to write these partial steps down. Finding a companion for life may seem to some just unachievable at some point in life. But perhaps finding ways to be more available to others, to go out socially more often, signing up for social networks (from a ballroom class to a match.com site), and telling everyone about being available and seeking the goal of finding a life companion, may all be easily achievable sub-goals.

It might also be helpful to make your goals public. Not only because people may then help you to achieve them. In addition, telling others about your pursuit makes it more likely that you will achieve it (e.g. stopping smoking).[88]

Goals should be achieved and finished to their fullest. Every single time you think “I should do this” or “I should try that” and then do not follow through and actually do it, the uncompleted action creates a little nagging but otherwise empty space in your mind. You’ll also miss out on the satisfying feeling that comes with the completion of a project. Be a finisher. Actually doing the things I set out to do, increases my level of satisfaction.

Regarding pursuing goals, rewarding people for what they already enjoy doing may undermine their enjoyment. It turns ‘play’ into ‘work.’ This may seem at first counterintuitive. For me, this may actually occur regarding writing. I do it expecting to make no money from it. If I did get money, it might become an activity I depend on for income, and take the ‘fun’ out of it. Kids who are rewarded for something that before was free play, tend to abandon the activity.[89]

As before, we won’t dwell much on the other side of the coin. But one should at least briefly consider what happens to people who do not have any goals. These persons have no direction, no passion to pursue, no incentives for action. They are usually lost, having no raison d’etre.

Finding a greater meaning

"Work is love made visible"

Kahlil Gigran

The fourth key to happiness is finding a greater meaning to what you like to do, to your perceived quest. Meaning is the belonging to something bigger than just yourselves. Having a successful career really just means that you've found a way to play that others are willing to pay for, because it is important.

Most people find meaning in their work. Work often requires us using our strengths at the top of our capacity, stretching our skills, with concentration often leading to flow, with clear goals, and chance for recognition. It is no surprise that often we may feel more engaged at work, than at home, where leisurely activity may not bring true happiness, but just short-term positive emotions.

You will spend most of the day in your job. Satisfaction with one's job makes people happier, as shown in innumerous studies. Who wakes up happier, and earlier: the one who has a purpose, or the one who has nothing to aim for? It is also true, if on the one side having a good job increases happiness, the relationship exists also from happiness to good job, as happier people tend to gain more enjoyment from their work.

This is the difference between having a job, versus a career, versus a calling.[90] Callings are traditionally those of priests, physicians, scientists, teachers, court justices.[91] In fact, religious work is often the one associated with the most happiness, probably because it is a calling, not 'just a job.' Interestingly, the number 1 and 2 most trusted professions are doctors and teachers, respectively.[92]

As I am a physician, in particular a maternal-fetal medicine specialist in high-risk pregnancy, let me explore medicine in more details. Medicine is not a job, which you just show up only because you have to. Or a career, where you enjoy the pay raises, and maybe some name recognition. In a career, when the promotions, or pay raises, stop, alienation starts. Medicine is, and should be, a calling.

For me, obstetrics, which involves helping women have healthy pregnancies and healthy babies, is a calling. I spend time with women who are or want to get pregnant, who believe in life, who create new life. I take care of high risk pregnancies, where either the mother or the fetus are sick, or have problems.

I would definitively continue to work towards improving the health of pregnant women and their babies even if I had to do it for free. Several times I've wondered if, given the situation, I would even pay for the gratification to do what I do at work. We are lucky, as what we like to do, coincides with saving lives, and improving people's health. Our efforts are therefore of great value to others, and to society; they bring respect.

Not only can a health care worker have a direct effect on her own patients. One can also make a big difference worldwide. I can affect the fate of the 130 million annual births in the world. By contributing to the research and the guidelines for management on pregnancy disorders, I can affect hundreds of millions of lives.

Over 300,000 mothers still die in pregnancy in the world every year, but this is down from over half a million. Millions of babies still die every year before their first birthday, but this rate has gone down significantly. As my focus is also the prevention of preterm birth, or trying to avoid the baby being born too early and therefore risking life-threatening complications, I'm happy to report that the incidence of preterm birth has decreased by over 10% in the last 5 years in the US, and is decreasing also globally. I'm not delusional enough to think it's all because of my efforts; but I like to think I've contributed. A physician scientist can affect the global management of any disease she does research on. The responsibility is enormous.

Doctors are an easy example, but, as we have reviewed, any occupation can be perceived as having higher meaning. Even janitors, when they can see that their work can improve other people's lives, can consider their job as a calling. Even cleaning vomit or bed pans in a hospital can be associated with gratification and happiness, if the employees identify themselves as part of the team who is healing people.[93]

A third of administrative assistants expressed their work as a job, a third as a career, and a third as a calling, depending on what potential meaning they placed on what they do, even if what they did was nearly exactly equal to their peers. We should all rewrite our job description so to highlight the higher meaning we can find in what we do at work.

The more we can align our daily tasks with our personal vision, the more likely we are to see our work as a calling, and the happier we'll be. The fastest way to disengage an employee is to tell her that her work is meaningful only because of her paycheck.[94]

Doing good is doing high-quality work which is beneficial to others. Doing well is professional achievements, and rewards. When doing good leads also to doing well, happiness follows.[95]

On the other hand of the spectrum, despite the fact that they make the most money (at least in the US) compared to any other professions, lawyers are the most unhappy.[96] They are surrounded by broken marriages, criminals, theft. Lawyers need to be aggressive, judgmental, and emotionally detached; they have high stress, do better if they are pessimists, and therefore suffer depression (3.6 more times than the average employed person),[97] and even mental health issues.

Obviously meaning can be found in activities which are not strictly one's employment. Einstein did his best research while working as a clerk in a patent office. Gregor Mendel did his famous genetic experiments as a hobby. Ben Franklin also did his best work outside of a defined 'job.' We often do our best work when we can have more uninterrupted time on what we like to do best.

To find a greater meaning, it helps to dream big. Several of the great scientific discoveries were made by young men who dared what seemed as the impossible at the time. Einstein discovered the theory of relativity when he was 25 years old. DeBakey invented the pump for the artificial heart at 23. Watson discovered the structure of DNA at 24. This list could continue for a few pages.

Nonetheless, dreaming big is something which can be done at any age, and in fact should be a lifelong activity. The heart-lung machine which still saves thousands of lives every year was first successfully used at Thomas Jefferson University, where I work, by Doctor John Gibbon, who was 50 at the time. Relish the difficult. And do not be afraid: if you want to make no mistake, then you'll do nothing.

So a meaningful life is one that aims at something larger than we are. Another benefit of this pursuit it that it might help make us feel closer to our fellow humans, whom we are helping. And also, for some of us, closer to a higher being.

As teenagers and then young adults, humans spend a lot of time pondering and eventually deciding on two choices: 'Which mate,' and 'Which job.' In this order, I think these two may be the most important decisions in one's life. Happiness research does confirm that social interactions and the capacity to get to flow doing something we enjoy, are two paramount keys to well-being.

Interestingly, scientists have likened humans to plants. Like plants need soil, sun and water to grow, humans need two main ingredients, apart from their physiological needs: love and work. When Freud was asked what a normal person should be able to do well, he said, "Love and work."[98] Leo Tolstoy wrote, "One can live magnificently in this world, if one knows how to work and how to love, to work for the person one loves and to love one's work."[99]

Working hard

"Happiness is not just a mood – it is a work ethic"

Shawn Achor

The fifth key to happiness is working hard. Some happiness experts have called this 'engagement,' describing the absorption of an enjoyed yet challenging activity.[100] When you are doing what you love, you want to do it as hard as you can. Great achievers are not trying to please an unpleasant parent; they are trying to satisfy a curiosity that burns inside them. This might include a desire to win, to get to the goal first, to beat the competition, but the enthusiasm is of a healthy competitive spirit. They work hard because they want to.

The successful people you admire are often those who practiced the hardest, as per the famous 10,000 hours rule of Malcolm Gladwell.[101] Practice is a means to gain freedom, and to develop talent. Think about the Beatles. They played for eight hours straight in Germany, every day, when they were still a young and unknown band from Liverpool. Think Michael Jordan. Think Roger Federer. Think Beethoven. They worked constantly. Their whole life was dedicated to practicing their skills, and constantly improving.

Clearly, such performers start by doing what they like. Some of them practice active forms of leisure, as 'working hard' does not mean exclusively 'at something related to one's employment.' They play for fun initially. They are at some point in flow. They love the music, the sport, the task, and practice all the time. Then they begin to get praises, and that stimulates more practice, and more practice, which leads to mastery, which leads to recognition, which leads to happiness.

No matter how much talent one has, she has to work her butt off to excel. One of my mottos is: 'the harder I work, the luckier I get.' It has worked all my life. Emulate the best, the ones who work the hardest for their happiness. Competition is a good thing. When you are with the best, this pushes you.

One of the keys to being happy is being able to suffer a defeat, but to never lose heart. I got the first B's of my life the first year of medical school. It was a rude awakening. I finally realized I could not do it all myself. I needed to work with others, and play to my strengths.

For me, an example of hard work, and mastering something with the help of a big team, was when I saw my first medical textbooks published, and selling. The feeling of mastery pushes us to want to do more and more. You become self-motivated. You do not need external motivation, from parents, partner, colleagues, friends. The motivation comes from your own realization that working hard at something you are good at - your strength - has significant benefits, which matter to you directly. People like to do what they do well.

From mastery, comes also optimism. Optimism is the tendency to believe that there is always a realistic solution, that there is always hope, no matter how difficult things are or seem. People who make permanent and universal explanations for good events are happier. Those who make temporary and specific explanations for bad events more easily bounce back from setbacks.[102] Salespeople with optimistic 'explanatory style,' as it's called, sold 37% more insurance than pessimistic ones. Learned optimism predicts how well students do in high school, recruits in military academy, athletes in sports, and patients after coronary surgery.[103]

What happens once the goal has been realized? You do feel some sadness. I felt it when I got to Professor, when I got Tenure, when I became President of the Society for Maternal Fetal Medicine (SMFM). You think, "Hooray! Fantastic!" and soon after, "So, what do I do now?"

When it comes to goal pursuit, it is really the journey that counts, not the destination. Happiness comes more from making progress toward the goal, than from achieving it. I almost do not want the writing of this book to end, as I enjoy it so much. Shakespeare said, "Things won are done; joy's soul lies in the doing."[104] But you need to force yourself to celebrate it, and to enjoy it. In time, new goals develop.

Recognition

"You did not just do better than myself. You left me in the dust you did so well!"

Andrea Berghella (my father)

The sixth, and last key to happiness, is recognition. This has also been called 'accomplishments,'[105] as it involves having realized tangible goals. It is the 'pat in the back.' It is the feeling of being valued by others, especially others whose opinion the person respects. Most adults can remember a teacher who inspired them to do excellent work, whose opinion the child really cared for, and who praised the child at the right moments, for the correct behaviors and achievements.

Giving a person responsibility, empowers them. Once you know that your task, your actions, matter to people who matter to you, then what you do becomes more uplifting to you. This has another important consequence. You feel more closely connected to the people who have praised you. This recognition builds the bridge from mastery, back to connectedness.

Personally, becoming a doctor allowed me to get praises from people I highly admired. This started probably from my dad, and later on from my mentors. When you learn to do something well, and someone else values this achievement of yours, you feel not only a sense of personal pride, but also a feeling of being associated with the person you idolized and now is recognizing what you have done. You feel a sense of connection with the whole organization, or profession.

In my case, a physician has connection with the individual patient, whom you have treated effectively, and with compassion: she will never forget you. You have her recognition forever. I have received, and saved, hundreds of "thank you" notes. Recognition is a natural validator that what we are doing has worth. This then motivates you to want to do more.

I also feel a sense of connection with all ob-gyn physicians and healthcare workers, and with all 130 million women who carry a pregnancy every year in the world. The best recognition of all is personal: the feeling that you have accomplished a personal goal, one important for yourself, which you had set up a long time ago and was hard to achieve.

Interestingly, at my stage of career, my colleagues and I judge our individual success by how one contributes to the success of others. The professor who best promotes the academic success of her mentees gets the highest recognition. In my profession, we as colleagues are judged by how many great mentees we have helped find and use their own strengths.

Of course, do not let recognition go to your head. I get reminded of that every Wednesday evening, when my wife asks me to take out the trash. We doctors do feel superhuman at times, not because of our abilities, but because of the privilege we have in helping others. Family and friends should help bring us back to reality. I thank Paola for being the best co-pilot I could ever have.

Other intentional activities associated with happiness

People do not realize what makes them happy. For example, they move to California or Florida for the weather, only to find themselves not happier than they were before. They buy a Ferrari, but still after a few days they are not happier than before. They switch jobs to get more money, only to find out they hate the new job. As their income raises, people get used to the higher standard of living, and soon feel like they again need even more money to lead a good life.

Over the last few decades, scientific research has disproven some common myths, as the ones above, and found many other activities, which we can somewhat influence, associated with one's happiness level. Much of the data has come up with similar, consistent findings.

For example, research by John Robinson and Steven Martin revealed that things that give us happiness include socializing with relatives, socializing with neighbors, and socializing with friends, working, having sex, going to a religious service, and reading a newspaper. According to others, the six most important factors associated with happiness are social relationships, marriage, employment, perceived health, religion, and quality of government. [106] Others list the keys to happiness as job, trust, social interests, faith, married, helpful stable government.

For our purposes, I think it's essential to review these not only in order of importance (the six most important already reviewed above), but also from the ones we can most affect by our own choices (e.g. social relationships), versus the ones we have less or little influence on (e.g. the quality of our government).

Pleasures

Pleasures are delights which have clear sensory, and strong emotional, components.[107] Touching something soft, smelling a nice aroma, tasty foods, warm baths, dancing, seeing beautiful scenery (or a handsome person), hearing your favorite music, orgasm, are all pleasures.

They are usually short-lived, and provide a positive sensation, but not long-lasting happiness. They provide a positive emotion, and then fade rapidly. We also adapt to these pleasures. The first taste of a vanilla ice cream is the best. The fourth taste already brings with it the idea of calories.

Surprise can help keep the pleasure more positive. To avoid adaptation, spacing may also be beneficial: having sex all the time may make even this most pleasurable of experiences less thrilling. Too much ice cream all the time may lead to nausea. Savor your pleasures, slowly, and intermittently. Variety is the spice of life.

Pleasures can also be very different from person to person. In one of his movies, when discussing the frequency of sex, Woody Allen states sadly, "We hardly do it, 3 times a week." While talking with her friend, his lover Diane Keaton almost with disgust blurts, "We do it constantly, 3 times a week."

Pleasures are based on senses and emotions. It is important to distinguish them from gratifications, which are about enacting personal strengths and virtues. Pleasure is easy, and usually does not require much effort and motivation. Gratification often instead requires work, and can be demanding.

That is why we tend to sit in front of TV instead of reading our favorite book or engaging in deep conversation. We do not realize these latter activities are associated with gratification, which provide long-lasting well-being. Again, we tend to choose short-term goals, forgetting that the most reward comes from long-term enjoyments. In addition, pleasures do not make us wiser or better in the long run. Gratifications usually do, by challenging us to learn, improve, and achieve.

Marriage

Those who marry may be happier to begin with. Happy people marry sooner, and stay married longer, compared to less happy people, as probably they are more desirable as dating partners, and are easier to live with as spouses.[108] But marriage and the courtship leading to marriage often produce a significant increase in well-being.[109,110]

The increase of happiness level given by marriage is modest to high. Based on data from 16 countries, 25% of married people and 21% of singles described themselves as 'very happy.'[111,112] In another study, 40% of married adults called themselves 'very happy,' compared to 23% of non-married controls.[113] If the relationship works, "there are few stronger predictors of happiness than a close, nurturing, equitable, intimate, lifelong companionship with one's best friend."[114]

Some research has found that the increase in happiness level associated with marriage can be somewhat short-lived. The sense of well-being tends to return to prenuptial levels within 2 to 3 years,[115] or up to 5 or 6 years.[116] The peak of happiness given by a new partnership seems to be certainly in the first 18 to 24 months.

Passionate love does not turn into compassionate love. The two are different. Do not get married in the 6 to 18 months of passionate love, as this always ends, no matter how 'good' your partner is. Marry, if you want to, for compassionate love, when you know each other well and you trust each other, truly wanting to continue to grow together and share life as teammates.

There are ways to make the happiness boost from marriage last longer. Dedicating oneself to be the best partner one can be, and not taking the significant other for granted; saying often "I love you;" taking active interest in the other's life and needs; giving affection and caring with small and large acts of fondness;[117] these are the ways to make a relationship such as marriage continue to bear happiness rewards. You have to believe in and dedicate yourself to the rapport you have chosen.

Many worry about the demands of keeping their significant other happy, or having to compromise. But overall, balancing the duties versus the gained advantages of having a trusted and esteemed co-pilot, tips the balance certainly towards happiness.

Long-lasting happiness is not getting married, but staying happily married. That is the hard part. For example, there is a disconnect between the ID who looks at another girl (or boy) and wants to go to bed with her, and the Superego who knows that you have a wonderful relationship with your married partner.

Providing effective pre-marital counseling to make sure the partners are compatible and understand the proven keys to a successful life partnership could certainly be a way to increase individual and societal happiness. But overall, the happiest couples are those with positive, optimistic partners, who are able to see the bright side of their relationship, and focus on the strengths, rather than the weaknesses, of their partners. They even try to see some positiveness in the imperfections of their mates. The actor Robin Williams, in the movie Good Will Hunting, stated that one of the things he missed most of his wife was the fact that she farted in bed. Science shows that this kind of reasoning is deeply true.

The end of marriage leads to unhappiness.[118] On a 100-point scale, 5-8 points are lost for separation and/or divorce, with the effect lasting for almost 10 years.[119]

Perhaps one of the best effect of marriage (usually a happy marriage, that is) on happiness is on the children. Even controlling for income, education, and other factors, children who grow up in a household with two married parents have better school performance, fewer emotional and behavioral problems, less substance abuse, less criminal activity, and fewer out-of-wedlock births.[120]

In another study, compared to children with other parenting arrangements, children of married adults living together:[121]

- Got better grades;
- Repeated grades at one-third to one-half the rate;

- Got treated for emotional disorder at one-fourth to one-third the rate;
- Got less depression;
- Matured more slowly sexually;
- Had more positive attitudes toward potential mates;
- Were more interested in long-term relationships.

Employment

Satisfaction with one's job makes people happier, as shown in innumerous studies.[122,123,124] Trust in management has a great effect on happiness, far more than income.[125] It is also true, if on the one side a good job increases happiness, the relationship exists also from happiness to good job, as happier people tend to gain more enjoyment from their work.[126]

Most people consider their jobs to be more pleasant than unpleasant.[127,128] Those who see their work as a calling find what they do to be fulfilling and socially useful. They do not work for the money or for the career advancement, but because they want to. As we have seen, teachers, doctors, nurses, scientists, artists, and others may be more likely to enjoy their work and believe that what they do for a 'living' makes the world a better place. Even hospital cleaners, though, if they see their work as leading to improve the health and happiness of others, can consider their job a calling, and therefore be happy with it.[129]

A calling is the most satisfying form of work because, as a gratification, is done for its own sake, rather for any material benefits it may bring. Enjoying the state of flow which accompanies a calling-type of work should become the principal reason for working.

It's interesting that, if one can find engagement, meaning, and accomplishment at work, most of the important activities associated with happiness can be found on the job. Social interactions of some importance can be found at work, but are mostly best outside of work. Pure pleasure activities do not occur mostly at work.

For me, obstetrics is a happiness profession. We spend time with pregnant women, in their prime of life, and witness the birth of new life. Not only this unforgettable, always emotional event makes the woman and her family happy, but also everyone else involved is overwhelmed with joy.

Workers who are afraid of losing their jobs are likely to be less happy, more likely to have sleep disorders, depression, and decline in perceived health.[130] Nonetheless, shielding individuals from this risk too much does remove their responsibility, and ultimately saps the vitality of the nation.[131]

Losing one's job is associated with 6 points less on the 100-point happiness scale, with associated loss of self-esteem, fear of losing the respect of others, higher likelihood of suicide, depression, and drugs or alcohol abuse.[132] Interestingly, unhappiness among employees who have been laid off tends to diminish somewhat if the level of unemployment in the community is high, or if other members of the family are also out of work.[133] Misery loves company.

Declaring bankruptcy or losing one's home and having to live on the street is devastating on the level of happiness, second in effect only to death of a child.[134]

Perceived health

Self-reported health is more important in regards to happiness than just health as rated by a doctor, because it includes stress, social isolations, and depression.[135] Only a few afflictions take a grave and lasting toll on happiness, and these are chronic pain, depression, and fatal disease such as cancer.[136]

Otherwise, even the loss of a limb, or becoming a quadriplegic, is usually associated with regaining of the former level of happiness within a year![137] Paralysis, or blindness, or other conditions involving a major loss of function, seem to be temporary setbacks, and not associated to lower happiness, because of our remarkable human ability to adapt to the most difficult of situations.[138]

This is the good side of adaptation. For example, people kidney problems, who perceive them as manageable, are as happy as healthy adults. Even dialysis patients, who have to be hooked up for hours several times a week to a machine to survive, show similar levels of happiness compared to healthy controls, when beeped randomly during the day and asked the mood they were experiencing at that very moment.[139] These kinds of data are indeed an excellent indicator of well-being, because they are unfiltered by recall. They ask about satisfaction right at that moment.

Exercise is well-known to contribute to happiness. In the short term, it increases endorphins which improve mood. In the long term, even for school-age children, as well as for any age individual, exercise improves mental alertness, school and work performance, health, longevity, while decreasing stress, anxiety, depression, and obesity.[140]

I am so much happier when I have finished swimming, compared to before. While the 40-minute swim in itself is not that enjoyable, the ensuing improvement in mood is tremendous, and lasts many hours, with even longer beneficial effects. This is another example of being able to delay happiness for bigger gratification later. Related to health, being of normal weight, by having a healthy diet, contributes to happiness. Sleep is also important. Having a bad night's sleep affects well-being the next day far more than having little money.[141]

Altruism

Performing acts of kindness to others, in and of itself, as we would want to receive them, is associated with a significant increase in levels of happiness.[142] In a study, two groups of people were given some money with instructions to spend it all in the next 24 hours. You like this study, ah? One group was randomly selected to spend it on themselves, while the other was selected to spend it on others in need. A day or two later, those who gave to others tested to be significantly happier than the control group who used the money on themselves.[143]

Volunteering, which is clearly an altruistic activity, is also associated with a substantial increase in well-being. It is proven that volunteering makes people happier; and also that happy people volunteer more.[144]

We all can be divided roughly into three kinds of people, as reported by Susan Dominus in an interesting New York Time article in 2013, and described originally by Adam Grant, a professor at Wharton School, in Philadelphia. These include takers, matchers, and givers.

Takers seek to come out ahead in every exchange. The lesson for non-takers is to collaborate, offer help, grant the favor, to pretty much anyone who asks, except maybe for the few proven takers.

Matchers give only when they can see that they can get in the future something in return of about similar value, from someone who can help them.

Givers give without expectations of immediate gain. They are generous, just for the sake of donating. They are happier than non-givers. Interestingly, givers can be great achievers and leaders, as giving motivates them. Givers in the end often win, because of their attitude: "Everything I do always comes back to me." But some can also end up as doormats who go nowhere and burn out.

The most successful givers are strategic in their giving, i.e. they give to other givers, or at least to matchers. They also consolidate their giving into chunks, as they know that combined giving yields more happiness.

Success can be described also as assisting others in their achievement. It is a selfless act of giving. Success should be described not just by what you have, but most importantly by who you are and by what you do with your internal gifts. Success is what you make of yourself and how you use yourself to contribute to the life of others.

Giving also allows the great reward of being remembered, and being remembered in a positive way. As the greater use of a life is to spend it on something that will outlast it, giving and therefore being remembered is a very effective way to have a successful life. Donating (time, $, etc) makes people (the 'donor' especially) happy. Andrew Carnegie stated, "The man who dies rich, dies disgraced."[145] Be a giver.

There is a Buddhist prayer, recited by the Dalai Lama, which goes:

May I become at all times, both now and forever,
A protector for those without protection
A guide for those who have lost their way
A ship for those with oceans to cross
A sanctuary for those in danger
A lamp for those without light
A place of refuge for those who lack shelter
And a servant to all in need.

These data to me are one of the best prospects for the future I could hope for. If we'll follow what the data show, to be happier we'll do more for others, and gain satisfaction for doing so. I surely hope we'll rise to this challenge, which will improve not only us individually, but the whole world.

Ability to deal with adversity

People need adversity, setbacks, at least challenges to reach their highest possible levels of strength, fulfillment, and personal development.[146] These benefits are called 'posttraumatic growth.'[147]

This large body of research reveals that rising to a challenge, and being able to bounce back from difficulties, is what reveals your hidden abilities. Then, when you realize these unknown talents, this gives you better confidence, and strength, and positive emotion. After trauma, people in general realize they are much stronger than they expected. 'Suffering produces endurance, and endurance produces character, and character produces hope.'[148]

In addition, going through adversity, such as cancer, rape, fire, or hurricanes, often reveals the strength of our social support group. Family and friends rise to the occasion and help us out, making us feel their love, and stimulating our gratitude back.

Finally, after trauma we often change our priorities, our goals, and adopt a different philosophy about life. These are turning points, which help us realize our true goals in life, away from materialism, into caring for others and strengthening our social relationships.[149] Often people decide to dedicate themselves less to a 'job,' and more to their calling, their loved ones, their favorite activities.

In adversity, those who talk more with their friends and their support group are largely spared any possible health-damaging effect of trauma.[150] Get it off your chest. Share the temporary pain, difficulty, stress, with others. It will help make sense of the negative event, and develop a deeper insight which generates personal progress.

I realized in medical school that even when I worked as hard as I possibly could, someone would almost always do better, even studying a bit less. That taught me a lesson, for sure. I was not the best, or invincible, as I was perhaps in elementary, middle, high school, and college. But I soon realized that if I steadily did well in all I liked, I could still do well overall, and that one does not always have to come in first to succeed.

In fact, it's important sometimes just to participate, do ok, and be nice, to be given opportunities. I learned that it's important to be able to suffer a defeat, but never lose heart. Getting scientific manuscripts rejected, and grants denied, only made me better, able to later do better research, and get bigger awards, if that was what I still really wanted.

Religion

Being religious is associated with a gain of 3.5 points on a 100-scale of happiness.[151] Forty-one percent of Americans with 'strong' religious beliefs are 'very happy', while only 31% of Americans who are only 'somewhat' or 'not really' religious are 'very happy.'[152] Deeply religious people tend to have better health and longer lives, and are also less likely to commit crimes, get divorced, or kill themselves.[153]

There are several reasons why being religious contributes to happiness, and these have to do with what being religious usually implies. First, religious beliefs add a sense that one's life and work have a purpose and meaning which make them seem worthwhile.

Second, religion can also be a surrogate for being altruistic, and the benefit of helping others. Being religious often involves doing acts of charity, and community service, which are all activities associated with happiness. The happiest people tend to do more for others, and gain satisfaction from doing so.

Third, and just as important, going to church, and being involved in religious activities, means these persons have added social relationships, which, as we have seen, are the number one key to create happiness.

Quality of government

Many aspects of the quality of the government one resides in can have a significant impact on personal happiness. This factor may be under a bit less of our control than the ones we have examined so far, but we can still affect it, by getting involved in politics or at least in community activities, by voting, or by moving to a place with better government.

Interestingly, it is true that good government makes happy people, but, even more, than happy people have a big effect on the quality of their government,[154] once again emphasizing the fact that we can indeed have a significant effect on our environment.

Living in a democracy which guarantees personal freedom is associated with happiness. In fact, freedom was the most potent factor in the rise of happiness in countries in a recent study.[155] All happiest countries have been democracies for more than 80 years.

Observance of the rule of law, efficient government agencies, low level of violence and corruption, high degree of trust in public officials (especially the police), tolerance of minority groups, all are associated with greater happiness. Greater tolerance of gays and other minorities increases national happiness.[156] Unfortunately, this explains why my country of origin, Italy, is ranked 45th in happiness.

There are many agencies which compare countries in terms of 'happiness.' The Legatum Prosperity Index is based on a study of 142 countries comprising 96% of global population. Nations are analyzed and ranked on 89 indicators in 8 categories such as education, government and economics. Per capita Gross Domestic Product (GDP) — basically how rich a nation is — is a factor in the index, but the whole point of the Legatum study is to look beyond such a simple measure at all the myriad issues which make up well-being and prosperity. In general, the 'happiest' countries enjoy stable political institutions, a strong civil society with freedom of expression, good education and healthcare, personal freedom, and a feeling of being safe and secure. Here is the 2013 ranking:

1. Norway
2. Denmark
3. Sweden
4. Australia
5. New Zealand
6. Canada
7. Finland
8. Netherland
9. Switzerland
10. Ireland

11. Luxemburg
12. United States

In the World Happiness Report of 2013, where 156 countries are ranked for happiness, the top five countries are Denmark, Norway, Switzerland, Netherlands and Sweden.[157] No matter which other institutions perform this survey, and even varying the factors surveyed, Scandinavian countries have for years come out on top.

Norwegians, for examples, have a stunning per capita GDP of $57,000 a year, and the second-highest level of satisfaction with their standards of living: 95% say they are satisfied with the freedom to choose the direction of their lives; an unparalleled 74% say other people can be trusted. If one looks at the list above, it is clear that a warm climate does not have much to do with happiness.

The variables responsible for over 75% of the international differences in average life evaluations per the World Happiness Report are, in order of importance, social support (having someone to count on in times of trouble), GDP per capita, years of healthy life expectancy, freedom to make life choices, prevalence of generosity, and perception of corruption.[158]

These factors relate to four issues: social, economic, psychological, and ethical. Social support relates to social. GDP per capita relates to economic. Years of healthy life expectancy relates to psychological and economic. Freedom to make life choices relates to all four. Prevalence of generosity relates to ethical. And perception of corruption relates to social and ethical issues.[159]

For the US, for example, rising personal income in recent decades has been offset by falling social capital, leading to a small slide in happiness rank from 11 to 17 in the World Happiness Report 2013.[160] All 16 countries happier than the US have lower income per capita, except for Norway.

While some of you may disagree based on your political and

social views, there is evidence that governments contribute to their citizens' personal well-being when they promote universal health care, availability of child care, paid parental leave, good and affordable – preferably free – public education, personal freedom coupled with safety in the community, a fair and meritocratic system for hiring and for professional promotion, antidiscrimination laws, help for the handicapped, and rules to protect the environment.[161]

Confirming that work is happiness, rising unemployment was responsible for a third of the drop in life evaluations seen in Southern European countries (Spain, Portugal, Italy, and Greece) between 2007 and 2013.[162] People enjoy great satisfaction when they know (or believe) that they live in a just world where hard work and good behavior pay off.[163]

'Your better life index' ranks countries according to 11 measures of well-being. As everyone has a different idea of what happiness looks like, you can change parts of the index according to your values, and recalculate. For example, if work-life balance and the environment are most important to you, Denmark and Sweden rank the highest. If income and health are most important, USA and Switzerland come up on top.

Many other societal changes which can be affected by politicians and which can boost individual happiness levels are reviewed in detail in 'The politics of happiness,' by Derek Bok.[164] Politicians should promote these issues, which will then help each of us find happiness.

Interesting, for the US, some of the happiness may come from the fact that the immigrant is someone who is pursuing a goal, and therefore he is happier to begin with. In fact, two novelty-seeking alleles of a gene called DRD_4, associated with the dopamine receptors in the brain and with exploratory behavior, are found more often the further one gets from where mankind started, Africa. Studies of the $_5$-HTTLPR gene, related to serotonin transport, have yielded similar results. So, for the US, being happy may simply be secondary to the fact that many of the most goal-oriented, and therefore happier people from all over the world, came here to work hard to follow their dreams.

On the other end of the spectrum, the country with the least happy citizens is in many surveys the Central African Republic (CAR). There the per capita GDP is $790 per year, and life expectancy is 48. Right behind the CAR at the bottom are Congo, Afghanistan, Zimbabwe and Haiti. In the World Happiness Report 2013, the bottom five countries (152 to 156) are Rwanda, Burundi, CAR, Benin, and Togo.[165] These countries have in general very low levels of freedom and safety, and high levels of unrest, violence, and significant poverty, causing daily stress. The gap between the top five countries and the bottom five countries is quite large, as per the World Happiness Report: 7.5 versus 2.9 on a 10-point (highest possible happiness score) scale.

Bhutan, the small country in the Himalayas, in Asia, has taken the lead in having its national laws and policies be guided by happiness criteria. Bhutan was the first to develop a Gross National Happiness (GNH) index, coined by their fourth king about 30 years ago. GNH was devised as a better alternative to the Gross National Product (GNP).

There are 4 parts to Bhutan's GNH: 1. Sustainable economic development; 2. Conservation of the environment; 3. Preservation of culture; and 4. Good governance. According to research done in Bhutan, they follow nine components of happiness: 1. Psychological well-being; 2. Health; 3. Time use; 4. Education; 5. Cultural diversity and resilience; 6. Good governance; 7. Community vitality; 8. Ecological diversity and resilience; and 9. Living standards.

Eventually every decision by Bhutan's government goes through consideration of GNH. For example, when considering a new tax or policy, the government will assess if it will increase or decrease GNH. 'Happiness economics' suggests that measures of public happiness should be used to supplement more traditional economic measures when evaluating the success of public policy.

After Bhutan's lead, now many countries survey their

citizen's happiness levels, and enact policies aimed at improving it. These nations include, among many others, Brazil, New Zealand, South Africa, UK, US, Australia, Singapore, and South Korea. International Gross National Happiness (GNH) conferences have met regularly in the last few years.[166]

Factors with modest impact on happiness

Studies have found that factors like money, education, or even having children do not affect happiness the way one might expect.

Money

Money is correlated with happiness, but only to a certain point. Average levels of happiness in the US are higher as one moves up the income scale. Clearly, for the many with a salary below $80,000 a year, and especially for those living around or below poverty levels, a higher income would bring more happiness.

Graph: Positive affect in relation to household income

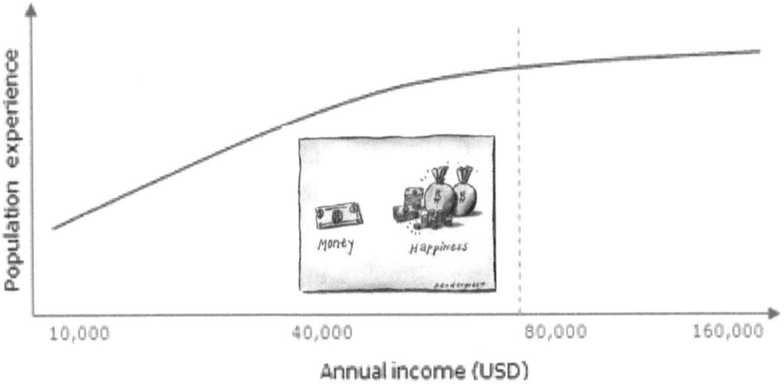

In the US, for example, 41% of people in the top quarter for income are 'very happy,' compared to 24% in the bottom quarter. Only 6% of top quarter people are 'not too happy', compared to 20% of bottom quarter people.[167]

As the graph shows, for many, a higher income would improve the level of happiness. We need to explain this association, too. The obvious reward is to be less stressed about saving, about not being able to afford something essential for themselves and especially for their loved ones, like good food, and a safe shelter. This concept relates to Abraham Maslow's pyramid, where at the base of happiness there are physiologic needs, and then safety needs, which both most often necessitate at least some money.

Interestingly, Americans are more than twice as likely (60%) as Europeans (29%) to believe that the poor can get rich if they only try hard enough.[168] Where you end up is a matter of luck and other circumstance for most Europeans, but only for the minority of Americans.[169] So lower income Europeans blame society, and are in general angry, while poor Americans are more inclined to think that wealthy peers must have deserved their fortunes.[170]

But with incomes over $80,000, happiness does not change any more. The salary needed for happiness is about $80,000 a year, or Euro 3,500 a month in Europe. This is called the Easterling paradox, named for American economist Richard Easterling, who first established that beyond a certain threshold, rising incomes don't bring happiness.[171,172] So, if one makes $350,000 or $150,000 a year, the level of happiness does not change just based on this difference in salary. It is true that, at a certain level, one cannot buy happiness.

There are several studies which confirm these findings. In another report, people's satisfaction with life changed little as their income increased or decreased, including the amount of pension.[173]

Another set of data, another way to look at this association, or lack thereof, is to look at national-level data. It is true that, in general, wealthier countries have happier populations than poorer nations, as shown above. But interestingly, when prosperity in a nation – especially if already prosperous - increases, the average level of happiness does not necessarily increases. For example, the levels of happiness in the US have changed very little in the past 50 years despite substantial increases in per capita incomes.[174]

Why isn't 'more money' associated with 'more happiness'? The more money you make, the more you want, as you begin to compare yourself to higher income people.[175] So the pursuit of financial goals is a treadmill in which people's aspirations are forever beyond their reach, leaving them perpetually dissatisfied.

People grow used to the extra possessions that higher incomes allow. Luxuries tend to become necessities, so that aspirations rise, leaving individuals no more satisfied with life than before.[176]

Happiness is all about how you compare. For example, you are very happy if you make $60,000 among friends who make less, but unhappy if you make a million but everyone around you makes more. Same for your house, wife, kids, car, clothes, etc. Satisfaction with one's financial situation depends in large part on how one's income compares with the income of others, in particular with those with whom one socializes.[177] When I compare myself to my good friends Marco, Tonino, Antonello, Corrado, Marco, Ignazio, Don, James, Francesco, and others, I feel happy, as I guess they make approximately what I make, and share my same values, which do not include at all greed.

This fact also explains why, as everyone in your social circle gets richer, including you, you do not get happier. Sadly, if others around you lose income, but you do not, you often might gain more happiness.

When given the choices of earning either: 1. $90,000 a year with coworkers earning $70,000; versus 2. $100,000 a year with coworkers earning $150,000, many choose option one, attesting therefore that the relative status of higher earner is worth $10,000.[178] People who care about other people's incomes are typically less happy with their lives.[179]

In fact, it can be that richer people are happier, not because of their higher incomes but because happier workers are more successful and earn more money. Students who were identified as happy in college earned 30% more by the time they were 40 than their classmates who were rated less satisfied when they were freshmen.[180]

Yet another aspect of happiness, as it relates to money, is that there are subtle rewards which come with being wealthy. These are recognition, higher status, feeling more successful because you get a free upgrade, the first seat at the opera or NBA game, invited to great events, and at times even fabulous parties.

Also usually being wealthy accompanies itself with having an interesting job, a challenging one, freedom of action, and again recognition (being the 'boss').[181] These people usually have more control on how they spend their time, and they are more likely to give orders than to receive them. They often have succeeded in what they were trying to achieve as young adults.

So, what is the message? What should you do? The happiest people among the well-to-do tend to be those who were never too preoccupied with financial success, but prospered by working hard at what interested them most, while managing not to sacrifice family and friendship along the way.[182]

What instead about becoming wealthy as a goal? Those who attach great importance to achieving wealth tend to suffer above-average unhappiness and disappointment.[183] People who value money more than other goals are less satisfied with their lives. They neglect the human relationships that affect their happiness.

The more people care about becoming rich, the less satisfaction they tend to derive from their family life.[184] Materialism distracts us from the most meaningful and joyful aspects of life, such as spending time with family and friends, and contributing to the community.

For example, 18-year old college freshmen at elite institutions who had expressed that making money was their primary goal, were less satisfied with their life two decades later compared to a similar control group who did not voice this materialist goal as primary.[185] So, aiming for money is associated with unhappiness (not happiness), with daily anxiety and anger,[186] and even with mental disorders.[187]

We know this is true. Almost 90% of Americans believe that 'our society is too materialistic,' and 84% agree that 'too much emphasis on money is a major problem for our society.'[188]

Interestingly, the happiest people are less likely to have the highest incomes. They are also less likely to be active participants in politics. They do not possess the extreme ambition to work exceptionally hard for worldly success.[189]

People who set as one of their most important goals getting rich tend to be less happy than those who have other goals.[190] I do not understand how so many people have getting rich as a goal, for the ultimate related purpose of eventually being able to 'veg out,' to take it easy, to hang out. Lifelong happiness does not consist of vegging out.

Part of the explanation of why so many people aim to get rich is that they have not understood what makes them really happy, or perhaps they have never thought about it in sufficient depth. Advertising, news, and the culture of our society in general makes them think, erroneously, that people are judged based on income, and possessions, so they accumulate these, often without finding any personal meaningful satisfaction once their economic goals are achieved.

Wealth growth in itself, either for the individual or the nation, is not an aim in itself, at least not when levels of above median affluence have already been achieved. The question is what to do with the attained freedom from economic worries. This liberty from money concerns should be used not to aim to accumulate more needless money, but to focus on the activities proven to increase happiness.

Education

In general, people with more years of education tend to be happier than people with less education.[191] This seems to be mostly due to the fact that people with more education learn enough self-discipline to develop healthy habits, and go on to get better paying jobs. Overall, more education is a factor, but not a major factors in people's level of happiness.

Having children

Interestingly, and to my surprise, having children, at least by research data, is associated with conflicting results regarding its effect on happiness. For many parents, their children are a source of joy throughout life.[192] My personal experience has been as such. My two sons have brought a tremendous amount of happiness to my life, as well as that of Paola, my wonderful wife and life co-pilot.

Wanting or not wanting to have children has a big influence. It's clear to all, and confirmed by research, that couples who want and cannot achieve parenthood go through periods, sometimes long-lasting, of unhappiness, compared to successful couples. Couples who instead choose not to have children are just as happy as couples who choose to do so.[193]

Other research has reported that having children is not always positive, and parenthood often fails to increase well-being significantly.[194]

The loss of a child, though, is usually the worst thing that can happen to someone.[195] And the resulting sadness, and depression, lasts for a while, often more than a decade, or a lifetime.

Factors NOT associated with happiness

Some of our activities and intentional choices make not much difference in terms of levels of happiness. This list will surprise you. Nonetheless, it is based, once again, on scientific research. Let's differentiate these factors between those one can, in general, control, versus those one cannot control. Let's start with those we have influence on, and we can choose.

<u>Can control:</u>

Geography and Climate

"When I'm in New York, I want to be in Europe, and when I'm in Europe, I want to be in New York."

Woody Allen

We cannot control the weather. But, in general, we can control where we live. Moving to a warmer climate has not been associated to affect the level of happiness.[196] So moving to San Diego from Buffalo should occur, in general, for reasons other than the 'better' climate, such as moving closer to social relationships with family and friends, or for a more satisfying job.

This is a hard one for me to swallow, as my mood is better in bright natural sunshine. But it is also true that the vast majority of the top 10 countries with the happiest populations do not have enviable seasons.

The fact that one of my former girlfriends would be unhappy just because it was raining, or cloudy, would drive me mad. We should not let the weather control our mood.

'Lying on the beach' is equated by many as the ultimate goal, as having reached happiness. This can be true if we mean by it having freedom from having to make money, being able to socialize with our friends, playing sports or just exercising and walking, or using the time to meditate. All of these are activities which bring happiness. But the weather does not have as much to do with the happiness of 'lying on a beach.' I want to be active even on a beach!

This fact that climate does not affect much happiness is due, in large part, to the phenomenon of hedonic adaptation.[197] We may be happy in a new, beautiful place initially, but we soon adapt to it, so that happiness is not affected for the better in the long-run. Hedonic adaptation has also a role on the happiness effects of wealth, chronic illness, shopping, a new car, a new house, girlfriends and boyfriends, and many other issues. We end up wanting more and more, and so run, and run, and run, towards ever bigger wishes, like hamsters on a wheel, unable to get anywhere, and especially unable to get to happiness. Happiness is not material. It is action. It is goals.

I have been told to have gone myself through major adaptation. I moved from college in New York to medical school in Philadelphia, back to New York for residency, and finally back again to Philadelphia for fellowship. My college girlfriend Beth, when she found out I had settled in Philadelphia, could not believe it. She remembered how much more I liked New York compared to Philadelphia when in college and medical school.

Watching TV

Compared to more active and more social forms of recreation, watching TV, and even going to the movies (unless dinner with friends follows), are associated with average or below average levels of enjoyment.[198,199] It is well known that watching TV more than one or two hours is in fact associated with poor mood, and depression. Forty-five minutes is probably plenty.[200] So stop doing it!

Shopping, buying something new

People adapt very quickly to the new acquisition. The dress longed for so long gives maybe a day, or two, of satisfaction. We adjust very quickly to the new status. Yesterday's luxuries become today's necessities, in a never ending, and especially never satisfying rush towards nowhere happy. Commercial advertising reinforces the continuous desire for more goods and services, emphasizing the joy they will bring; but this joy is almost over by the time we walk out of the shop.[201]

Recognize what you already have. Happiness at times resides more in learning to desire all that you have, instead of having all that you desire.[202] The more a purchase is motivated to impress other people, the least happiness it conveys.[203] Would you still engage in buying something even if you could not tell anyone, or show anyone else?

Can control a bit:

Physical beauty

Surprisingly enough, beautiful people are not happier than less-attractive controls.[204] Beautiful people are in general happy with their looks, but their happiness has minimal, if any, effect on their well-being. In fact, fashion models are less happy than their peers, probably because they are valued for their looks and have less meaningful social relationships.[205] Trying to look good at all costs limits your life.

Interestingly, the correlation between beauty and happiness is reversed. It is not beauty that brings happiness, but is happiness which makes us feel more beautiful. Happy people are more likely to perceive everything about their lives, including their appearance, in more positive, optimistic ways.[206]

We should also look at the long-term consequences of our choices, instead of just the short-term ones. We may look more attractive tanned, but over time we risk cancer, or at least just wrinkles. When tempted to get another portion of a delicious food, we should not just think about the short-term taste bud pleasure, but also about the long-term consequences of gaining weight and not feeling, or looking, our best.

Cannot control:

Gender

Being a man or a woman does not seem to influence one's level of happiness. Having a balanced work and family life is most important, not gender.[207]

Age

Age does not seem to have much of an effect on happiness.[208] Well-being declines slightly from a person's youth until about 40, and then improves gradually and slightly until the early 70's, and even later if health and interests are maintained.[209] So, contrary to popular belief, if anything, people get a bit happier with age.[210]

Some pessimists fear old age, and some less young people blame their age for their misfortunes. In a 1979 study of 75 year old individuals, some of them were sent for a week to a retreat center, where they were to pretend like it was 20 years earlier. Their IDs had pictures of when they were 55 years old, newspapers and magazines were from 1959, and everything, in short, was designed to make these 75 years old men feel like they were 55. Indeed, after the retreat, the men were more flexible, had better posture, hand strength, objective appearance (they looked 3 years younger), eyesight, intelligence, and memory.[211]

There seem to be significant benefits to believe we are younger than we are, both physically and mentally. In fact, when elderly people are reminded that cognition typically declines with age, they perform worse on memory tests compared to people without such reminders.[212] External reality, as we know, is malleable by our internal beliefs and sensations.

Winning the lottery

Adaptation has some remarkable effects on even seemingly major events which could make us happy or sad. Winning the lottery certainly brings initial joy. But, less than a year after this life-changing event, winners reported being no more happy than non-winners.[213] As we have seen, much addition of other physical things, such as clothes, presents, cars, and shopping in general, has to do with adaptation. You get a bigger house, but now live in a neighborhood where all houses are big, and begin to eye the even bigger ones, and the same happens with all other social comparisons.

Factors associated with unhappiness

Can control

Commuting

Commuting has consistently been associated with lower levels of happiness, particularly if commuting by car is long and in heavy traffic, when it is strongly associated with stress and unhappiness.[214] This is one factor to which we do not adapt.[215]

Household chores

Having to do household chores which you do not enjoy is associated with unhappiness, either if you are single or live with someone else.[216] These tasks may include doing laundry, having to go to the supermarket, cleaning the toilet or any part of the house, and even child care. Get someone else to do the laundry; it can be a leading cause for divorce.

Noise

Noise, especially if intermittent and variable, interferes with concentration and therefore flow. Consequently, it is associated with stress and unhappiness.[217]

Cannot control

Race or ethnic group

Unfortunately, being black is associated, in the US, with considerable less satisfaction with life than being white, even if this difference has gotten smaller in the last three decades.[218]

As you can see from this list, there are many myths in our society regarding happiness, and most are simply not true. You do not have to go somewhere (e.g. house in the suburbs, sunny climate, country, continent) to find happiness. Happiness is within. You do not have to go back to your youth, or middle age years. You do not have to surrender to your destiny, if you feel you were just born 'depressed,' as you can change your happiness level, 50% of it.

In summary, we need to stop complaining about our work, our boss, our partner, the weather, or other external factors. And we need to start doing the things which can truly help us to improve our happiness.

Childhood roots of adult happiness

"The child is the father of the man"

William Wordsworth

Connectedness. Play. Flow. Practice. Mastery. Recognition. Said in one line, without much of an explanation, these actions may not mean much to you. But, wait a few minutes, and, as you go through the next few pages, you'll see that these are the steps of the ladder that leads from a good childhood to adult happiness. A lot of the notions reviewed in this chapter are from concepts in the book 'The childhood roots of adult happiness,' by Edward M. Hallowell.[219]

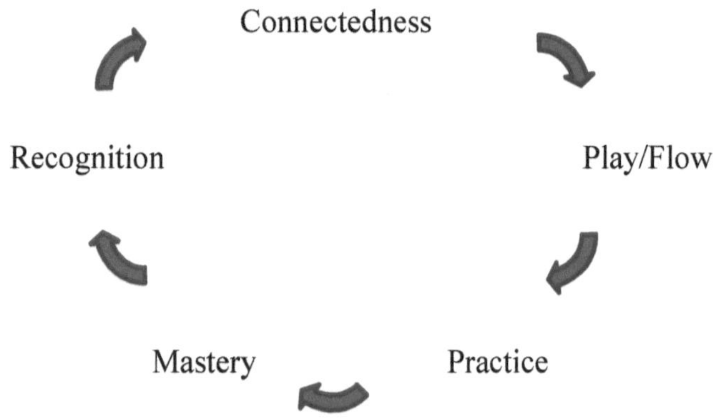

Connectedness

The most important of all these steps to reach happiness as a child, and then as an adult, is connectedness. The child should know that the parent is going to love her no matter what. Happy children know their parents love them no matter what, now, and always, forever.

The starting point in creating a connected childhood is unconditional love. This love is constant, unshakable, and totally reliable. It is the kind of love that gets incorporated in the person. The person receiving this love knows that this love will be always, always with him, will follow him anywhere, will never change, will resist any adversity. It is a secure attachment.

Humans get to happiness because of the connectedness they got as a child. Unconditional love should come from someone. Usually – but not always – this someone is a parent, or two parents. If not a parent, there must be a charismatic adult, e.g. grandparent, aunt, uncle, step-parent, or other, to inspire the child, to provide connectedness. You felt loved, no matter what.

Inner qualities such as resourcefulness, optimism, people skills, a can-do attitude, creativity, extroversion, a feeling of control over one's life, self-esteem, all come from connectedness, or at least can better manifest themselves when one is connected. And these are the attributes that in all research have been shown to be associated with happiness in life. Optimism in childhood correlated with optimism in adulthood. You feel understood, loved, wanted, paid attention to.

A parent's love is like the favorite stuffed animal our children carry around while they are young. Over the years it loses an ear or perhaps an eye, gains a few gashes that get repaired with tape, becomes faded and floppy, and all the while becomes stronger and stronger in the hold it exerts upon our hearts.

Touch is underrated. Our children necessitate to be touched more, to be given lots of frequent hugs and kisses. It is not enough to shake their hands. It is insufficient to put a red heart or another emoticon at the end of our texts, or emails, or tweets.

Think back about your own childhood, and what went well. For me, unconditional love came from my mother. In my mother's eyes I could do no wrong. Towards me, she had always smiles, praises, "you can do whatever you want," "you are the best." In middle school I wrote in one of my essays that my mother always said, "How can I have created such a beautiful, wonderful person?" Embarrassingly, my teacher told the whole class.

My own success in achieving happiness started for sure first from receiving, several times a day, wave after wave after wave, my mother's love. Unconditional and total affection was openly shown by her to me not only verbally and by touch, but also with action, and dedication.

I've at times felt invincible probably because my mother instilled her affection so deeply in me that I feel and carry with me her unconditional love everywhere. It is part of me, even if the original source is over 4,400 miles away. This unconditional love frees the person to be his own man. The love of my mother for me set me free to even leave her home and my home country. Moreover, if you received unconditional love, you are likely to be able to give unconditional love.

Thank your parent, or relative, for their unconditional love and support. Go ahead, do it. They may not be right next to you now, so do it later, but do not forget to give thanks. One of the best ways to do well in life is to have a secure, long-lasting attachment to one person, usually your mother, when you are very young.

While feeling connected at home is key, it is also important to feel connected at school. One should feel cared for, welcomed, treated fairly. Friendship, family, community, spirituality, love of nature, team play, are all forms of what is meant by connectedness.

Teachers in elementary, middle, and high school always believed in me. Initially, I was told I had terrible, tough, impossible-to-please teachers. Their last names were Mrs. Vizioli and Di Giovanni in middle school, and Filograsso and Di Daniele in high school. I'll never forget their names. I studied, I read, and enjoyed the hard work. I volunteered to do lots of extra math problems in middle school, as they were my favorite past-time, and I know I would make my teacher happy. Eventually I would excel with these teachers anyway, and become their favorite student.

Close relationship to a professor is key. So teach your child to get to know one faculty member reasonably well each semester, and also to get the faculty member to know her reasonably well.

This feeling of security and safety, this basic trust, instills courage and the desire and capability to take risks in life. An attitude of optimism is one of the strongest predictors of adult happiness as well as one of the most reliable protectors against depression and despair. You never feel alone. You feel strength from knowing that, even if failure follows your attempt, you have a trusted and reliable other person(s) to lean on, to count on for support, rather than being alone in a corner, in pain without support and comfort. Even if I feel lost, I always have someone to turn to. This gives confidence.

It is ok for children to experience some hardships, and even some moments of unhappiness. Life unfortunately will continue to subject us to such events later. The great danger for a child is not that, once in a while, he is going to feel bad about himself. The danger is not having ready, in the right place next to you, and at the right time just when it happens, a trusted person to talk to him about those feelings. It's not important that one has fallen down. The important issue is to get up, and be able to fight, or at least play, again.

The ages between 15 and 25, with first love, first big decisions such as college and job, living and traveling independently, and other 'firsts' and life-changing choices, are a special period for identity formation. Life events in this period have the most influence in the rest of our life story. Being able to face adversity in this period, and to overcome it in a positive way, with the help of a strong social support group, are most important.[220] When older people are asked to recall the most important events of their lives, most of the ones they mention occurred in this period.[221] Life starts to take shape by the late twenties, and adversity faced after this period is not as helpful.

Play

Play is one of the childhood roots of adult happiness. 'Play' here means any activity in which there is room for spontaneous invention and/or change. The opposite of play is doing exactly what you are told to do. Allow children to play. To find things they like to do, which make them go into 'flow.' Ask them what makes them go into 'flow.'

Happiness occurs when as an adult one finds a kind of play that people are willing to pay him to do. For me as an adult, a type of play is now writing. I can create, either for a science paper, or for a personal book. Happiness comes while I'm putting together a scientific manuscript, a chapter, a medical textbook, or while I'm composing a non-scientific book, usually non-fiction.

This is the scientist: an adventurer finding a way into unexplored worlds. That is why I like science. I love to look at data and let my brain go into flow trying to figure out what they are telling me.

Of course I'm lucky, as what I like to do coincides with saving lives, improving people's health, so with something that is of great value to others, and to society, as well as it brings respects and pays well.

The goal of a parent should be to help the child find his or her own domains of curiosity and desire, and then let curiosity and desire provide the pressure and determination and motivation. Finding something you love to do when you are a child is one of the keys to happiness in adult life. If, when you grow up, people are willing to reward you to do the things you love to do, then you've got it made!

So when you are young, playing with toys brings joy. When you are an adult:

- Play with words = become an author
- Play with numbers = become a mathematician
- Play with chemicals = become a chemist

- Play with basketball = become an athlete
- Play with people = become a politician
- Play with ideas = become a philosopher
- Play with emotions = become a psychologists
- Play with clothes = become a fashion designer
- Play with drawings = become an architect
- Play with health problems = become a physician

To allow for aimless play, and free flow of the brain, the environment is important. That means that some things must be in the environment, and some should not. Parents must at time exclude some toys, and erect some barriers on some issues. For example, while some time with media is ok, too much is bad.

Regarding the environment which is best for a child to grow up in, it should be and feel safe. There should be no guns at home. There should be no easy access to tobacco, alcohol, and drugs. At school, parents should ensure that there is no bullying, and no prejudice. Life is what you are used to. If you are used to good, you continue to be good. And viceversa. Since childhood.

Also, content of the media is important. Watching the Discovery or History channel may be better than watching wrestling. It is also quite possible to play constructively while at the computer, or on the internet.

I can tell by Pietro's (my younger son) mood how much time he has been on the PlayStation. If he is still reactive, and in a good mood, he has played an hour, or less. If he has played more than two hours straight, he is intractable, in a bad mood, jumpy, testy.

Playing FIFA (the international soccer game) on the PlayStation can be formative, as he is definitively in flow. He is trading players, buying young soccer champions, discovering ways to win. I do not know how much is too much, but I do know that his mood deteriorates after two hours, and that cannot be good.

Rules and regulations should be discussed since they are very young. I'm talking since they are one, two years old. I often say that most of the basic adult values, such as honesty, and sincerity, are learned by about eight years of age. They are hard to acquire after. Happiness requires some structure, so there are fewer surprises. When a child gets structure in her life, raised consistently in an environment in which rules are clear and time for flow is plentiful, she becomes happier, healthier, and more successful at everything she does. Children want to know that there are right ways and wrong ways of doing something. They need to be shown why it is important to adhere to the given instructions.

What Edward Hallowell calls ‘human moments’ are also important, and should be part of everyone’s childhood to lead to a happy adulthood. Examples of human moments are seating around together at dinner, playing with a friend in the backyard, talking in the car while driving somewhere.

Sports can be the perfect environment for play. People usually have fun playing sports, especially non-competitively. They will therefore practice more and more, and success, which is part of happiness, will follow.

Play later in life is also when you develop a hobby, such as golf, tennis, knitting, reading a newspaper, writing, playing chess, collecting antiques, gardening. Having a good hobby or more than one is key to happiness. People do not always understand what will give them lasting satisfaction, and consequently fail to act accordingly.

Flow

When we play, we reach the state of mind that Mikaly Csikszentmihalyi calls flow.[222] In flow we humans are at our happiest. We forget where we are. We forget what time is it. We even forget who we are. The more a person can find activities in which she can get into a state of flow, the happier that person will be, day after day. Almost any activity, from riding a bike, to reading, to writing, to playing the piano, to playing soccer, or to doing gardening, can lead into flow.

Csikszentmihalyi said “it is not enough to be happy to have

an excellent life. The point is to be happy while doing things that stretch our skills, that help us grow and fulfill our potential. This is especially true in the early years: a teenager who feels happy doing nothing is unlikely to grow into a happy adult."

To reach a state of flow, there are certain helpful characteristics of the 'play.' First, the challenge inherent in the activity should match the skill of the person involved. Too much challenge, and one feels frustrated and defeated. Expecting to win at tennis against Federer is an exercise in failure. Too little challenge and you feel bored, like if you play tennis with someone much worse than you.

In a state of flow, you are one with what you are doing. One usually reaches a state of flow when both the challenge the activity poses and your skill at that activity are high. When high skill meets high challenge, flow is apt to occur. Teachers, coaches, parents should know this to be better able to educate effectively.

Second, you can control the activity, you know what is going on from moment to moment, you cannot get lost or overwhelmed. I can volunteer for the activities I like to do the most at the American College of Obstetricians and Gynecologists (ACOG), and do them with dedicated passion. I can also decline or at least delegate to other members of the team what I'm less interested in, and good at.

Third, you get immediate feedback on what you are doing. If you miss a shot, you can see it, and do better next time. If the sentence you write does not look that good, you can go back and fix it. If you score, teammates congratulate you. If you write a nice article, soon your colleagues commend your good work.

One should never forget, especially a parent, that a child at play is a child at work. Play builds the imagination. Playing with other children teaches skills of problem solving and cooperation.

As for play, which is related to flow, one must create a safe environment where flow can occur. For a child, the parent must provide that environment. Flow will usually follow naturally. Family also is part of the environment. Children who interact a lot with family members have more flow. On the other hand, a child without support can experience fear, shame, and embarrassment, which prevent play and flow.

When I'm concentrated and immersed into a task, that's happiness. Examples of flow for me are writing a book, writing an article, doing the result tables, calculating the statistics. Like it was when I was a teenager and I enjoyed, to everyone's surprise, spending hours doing extra math homework, given to us as volunteer work, with me the only one to do it. I hang out with my colleagues at one of my favorite professional societies, the Society for Maternal-Fetal Medicine (SMFM), not only because they are smart, but also because I can 'play' with them, and challenge myself.

Whatever the activity, it has captivated your mind completely, so that you are not aware of anything else, not even your own being. This is why one becomes aware of her experience of flow only in retrospect. Often, some noise, some distraction, their name being called, brings them back to reality.

It's very important to daydream. We chart our lives in our dreams. We figure out what we like, what we want, who we really are. Sustained play leads to dreams, and dreams to beliefs.

Interesting, when we are in flow, which is also when we are happiest, we do not realize it at the time. We may not recognize happiness when it's happening. I do though look forward to spending an evening with good friends, talking one-on-one with a family member, correcting a scientific paper, analyzing research data, writing, or playing soccer, as periods I know I have a high chance of going into flow. Few other things get me into flow.

Another important aspect of play is to try different ways to play. Since the child is young, it's important to help her discover what she loves to do, and then encourage her to do it. I tried to teach my sons Andrea and Pietro how to play almost any sport, from tennis to basketball, from hockey to soccer, from swimming to skiing, from bowling to chess. Even if I was not a master at the sport, or even really pretty bad at it (e.g. chess, hockey), I could still show them the basics when they were little. They were appreciative. It brought connectedness.

In the book 'Finding Your Element,' Ken Robinson and Lou Aronica discuss how children should be exposed to as many things as possible, to give them the best chance of finding what 'sticks' to them the best.[223] To help them identify the sport, or the occupation, or the hobby, which they like the most. So play with them every sport you can. Take them to a classical music concert, and to the opera. You never know what they are going to like.

Andrea and Pietro took piano lessons, chess lessons, swimming lessons, practiced formally soccer, basketball, tennis, chess, etc. For Andrea, soccer, swimming, and chess stuck. For Pietro, basketball, soccer, and chess, so far. Each activity the child gets to experience, is a seed that might grow into a lifelong pleasure, or even a passion.

A child should be told, especially if struggling to find what they like, that they are already smart, and that they just need to find out exactly what they are smart at. Parents and teachers should help children (as well as adults, really) to find sources of joy to which they can turn their whole lives. It's best if these are sources that can be accessible, safe, and satisfying.

The most difficult step is finding a kind of play which you both like to do and you are good at. Then wanting to practice, and becoming a master, will follow somewhat easily. A parent cannot have skills in all activities. It's good to make sure their children interact with other adults who have different skills, different jobs, and are good possible examples to follow.

Apart from exposing their children to as many different activities as possible, parents and teachers should start to notice the specific qualities of the child. Part of the adventure of parenting, and even more part of the adventure of growing up for the child, is discovering how their minds works, what they do well in, what they enjoy the most, what they have trouble with or are just not interested in.

A good book to read regarding this is 'A mind at a time,' by

Mel Levine. Each child is different. Even if two sisters get exposed to the same activities, they won't like the same ones. One will choose ballet, the other volleyball. We must help children identify the area they most like, not only the one they succeed the best in. Hopefully there is an area the child enjoys, and the parent and teacher can help the child make the connection between fun and an area of learning.

Personal emotion is the on/off switch to learning. The child should learn to be self-motivated into apprehending new skills. Focusing only on grades, takes us away from noticing what mostly excites the child. It may be that the child gets an A in English, and a B in drawing, but most enjoys drawing. Keeping up with drawing, to become an architect or a painter, or just as an hobby for a lawyer, is a key to happiness.

Be sure, as a parent, to see your child for what she really is, and not what you want her to be. She will be happy only being herself, by reaching her own goal, not by reaching the goals you wanted for yourself.

Good parents sometimes do too much for their children. Too much cheering. Too much of a presence, obsessive, to the point the child will never gain independence. Too much help, making life too easy, so the child has never to work hard to achieve something, and loses the knowledge of the key connection between dedication and success.

Parents should teach their children how to fish. They should not be continuously providing new, fresh fish. We as parents must avoid excessive 'spoon feeding,' and instead must teach how to be self-sufficient. The balance between being too caring and too demanding is not an easy one, but must be found. It might differ a bit depending on the child, on the parent, on the circumstance, on their interactions. But to learn to fish by yourself is essential.

Parents and teachers should help the child at 'play' to avoid some pitfalls. One of them is the fear to make mistakes. This is the most dangerous of 'learning disabilities.' Fear of making errors is what keeps people from reaching their potential. In a way, I feel this is what has stopped one of my colleagues from publishing more scientific papers. The fear is of not being good enough, of putting in print something that was not perfect. Perfection is the enemy of good.

Interestingly enough, family financial status does not seem to influence flow much. In fact, research from Csikszentmihalyi shows that children from the more affluent families tend to be more bored, less involved, less excited than less-well-to-do teenagers, and therefore spend less time in flow.

The prerequisite for happiness is to get fully involved in life. If one retreats to a life of pleasure and luxury but no real purpose, he or she loses out, in reality. So do not buy a new BMW for your high school student; that is bad education. No unlimited spending. They have to earn the chance at getting their dreams come true. As probably many of you have seen, spoiling your kids especially when they are young, i.e. less than 25 years old, only ruins their life. I know, it's really hard for parents to say 'no.'

It is hard not to let our children enjoy what we parents can offer them, what we always wanted. But the joy for the gift of a beautiful Ferrari which has not been earned with hard work will disappear in a few days, and will only leave the lesson that rewards come despite effort. Find a way so that, if you really can afford to buy them a beautiful car, they can truly deserve it. One day your children will thank you for it.

I'm in a state of flow often. I go to sleep daydreaming about my children, my great family. I wake up thinking about some research project or some scientific paper for work. Under the shower, at 6am, my mind is flying so quickly I'm not really aware I'm awake. I look forward to going to work and putting my thoughts down on paper. I rush trying to get to work as soon as possible, to have the most time to concentrate on my thoughts while writing them down. Make sure you make yourself like your work! Interestingly, most people find most of their flow at work.[224]

But I'm in flow also about issues not related to work. Right now I'm in flow. I'm working daily on this book. I think about happiness most of my day, including at work. Whatever I do, I try to relate to these issues. I was looking forward all day to coming home and having some quality time between my free-flowing brain concentrated on happiness and this keyboard.

Once you are doing something you like, you want to get back to it all the time. Whatever the activity, you get so caught up that you strongly look forward, almost salivate at the idea of returning to the activity that is giving you this prolonged joy. For me, sometimes this can also be a book. Recently, reading 'Far from the tree,' by Andrew Solomon, had taken the center stage in my mind, and I could not wait to go back to this book and read the next chapter.

Gratification pours on me when I can get back to whatever flow activity is captivating me. The task is challenging and requires skill. I concentrate. There are clear goals. I get positive feedback. I'm in control. My sense of self, time, and space, vanishes.

I concentrate during any free moment in the day about what to write next, how to analyze the data, what the results means, how to organize the discussion, and what to really conclude based on the new scientific information we have gathered. Basically I keep on 'playing' with whatever project I concentrate on for several days, anticipating how much fun it is going to be when I can get back to work on that favorite project, just like I'm doing now.

I have finally consciously realized, in my late forties, that the more I find myself in this state of mind, the happier I am as a person. Even if I'm away from the computer, I have fun thinking about the project. For example, yesterday, while driving back with my family from a state chess tournament our sons played at, while Paola was taking a nap and they were playing with each other in the back seat, I wrote down some thoughts on small pieces of paper.

Yes, I was driving. But I was also flowing. And I never want to miss my best ideas, which come when I least expect it. That is why I always have a piece of paper and a pen in my shirt pocket, right over my heart.

Prolonged joy depends on your ability to get creatively involved with something or someone for an extended period of time. This process, indeed, is similar to falling in love. You cannot think about anything else. Your whole being is magnetically possessed by the issue. You become enchanted, completely taken, swept away, energized, motivated, as never before. You walk around with a big grin on your face, you smile at everyone, even strangers, you are nicer to others, you are living strong and full. You are in love with it, and you can't wait to get back to whatever it is you are loving to do.

Creating a habit of finding strong interests, hobbies, activities which you deeply enjoy brings happiness. Sports, games, writing, engaging conversations, and others are common examples. Active leisure is more enjoyable than passive leisure, such as watching TV, but it usually requires more initial effort. Each of us needs to develop a passion.

Be aware, finally, that while you want to be in flow as often as possible, you get so much reward from it that it can be addictive. Do not forget others – spending time with your significant other, or child, or friend, or person in need – by being addicted to your flow activity.

Practice

When you are doing what you love, you want to do it as hard as you can. Great scientists are not trying to please an unpleasant parent; they are trying to satisfy a curiosity that burns inside them. This might include a desire to win, to get to the goal first, to beat the competition, but the enthusiasm is of a healthy competitive spirit, not a fear-driven, to lose-means-to-die attitude. They work hard because they want to.

One practices also because a key to happiness is to have control over yourself and your environment. One must understand, often by being shown first by others, that practice is a mean to gain freedom, and to develop talent. Practice must be seen as something with a purpose. Not as a meaningless sets of worthless repetitions. Happiness through practice includes the ability to tackle a problem and stick with it until it is solved. Part of happiness is a can-do, want-to-do attitude. Optimism is practice leading to mastery.

The kinds of practice and discipline that endure derive mostly from enthusiasm, desire, and devotion. Guilt, fear, forced obedience will not lead to practice which is linked eventually to happiness.

With practice comes also discipline. The word 'discipline' derives from 'disciple.' The disciples of Jesus (or Mohammad, or Moses, or Buddha) followed him not because they were forced, but because of something they believe would make them and the world better, because of enthusiasm. Sacrifices are made from the belief that they will lead to something positive. And practice also shows us how to receive coaching, how to find a good mentor, how to best receive help and teaching.

So we display discipline and hard work in areas we love, and we are interested in. I am very disciplined at work. I arrive early. I often leave a bit later than anyone else. I get up an hour or two earlier than the rest of my family on weekends, and write these personal books. I get to be in flow, in silence, with the beautiful morning light, every Saturday and Sunday. After watching me give a plenary lecture at the biggest international congress of obstetricians and gynecologists, my colleague Brian Mercer told me that I was 'laser focused.' I was certainly in flow.

On the other hand, I am not focused at all on house chores. I often cannot find my keys. I am in trouble if left alone to do laundry. I have a hard time remembering jokes, and remembering movies. Ask me about where a certain medical fact regarding pregnancy was first published, and I can probably tell you the journal as well as the year, sometimes the month.

Clearly, I am disciplined about what I love, and undisciplined about what I do not. I love my family. I love my job. I love medical science, especially as it relates to pregnancy, because I've studied for so many years and I can understand it. I love writing. I love going to conferences where I can learn something new and important, and also where I can present my own new data and get feedback from smart clinicians. I love to play soccer, and also to watch it on TV, but mostly highlights, to make it more time efficient.

The child should comprehend that the successful people they admire are often those who practiced the hardest. Think Elton John, or Beethoven. Clearly, such performers were at some point in flow. They loved the music, practiced all the time, wanted to feel their fingers on the piano over and over. Then they began to get praises, and that stimulated more practice, and more practice, which led to mastery, which led to recognition, which led to fame.

No matter how much talent one has, she has to work her butt off to excel. We are all aware of people with tremendous natural gifts, who squander them because of little practice. On the other hand, I'm a big believer, backed by scientific data, that dedication is one of the major keys to a successful life. I'm myself such an example. Coaches and friends, not only parents and teachers, need to reinforce to the child the long-term goals of mastery and recognition, and show him how there can be some fun in the short-term at times painful, repetitive practice.

I've always taught our two sons as well as my students to emulate the best. Few admire the homeless bum begging on the side of the street. Children like winners. They would like to be the best in school, the best at baseball, the ones with the most money, and fame. So I try to find them good examples to emulate. I push so that they compare themselves to the best in their class, not the worst. I do not allow them to justify their subpar performance on a test because, "Malcolm also got a C." I do not permit, "I threw the gum on the floor, as it's so dirty already."

Once you can make the connection that practicing your play leads to mastery and recognition, you cannot stop, and want to get more and more. Parents do not need to incentivize their children. Children now want to read, because it leads to good jobs. They realize that not reading may lead to them having a hard labor job. Bosses do not have to mandate goals for their employees, if the employees know that the more they work, the more they get recognized, such as with raises, or promotions, or jobs, or better opportunities.

During practice we also learn to deal with failure. We learn that we must accept occasional disappointment, as if we do not try, we cannot fail. So, as Thomas J. Watson said, "To increase your success rate, double your failure rate." Learning anything is hard work, and requires a few mistakes. Saying things like, "I could have done better," or "I am a klutz," are part of the process of reaching mastery. The road to mastery is filled with mistakes and frustration. The important thing is to be able to look past the short-term hills, and concentrate on the long-term lofty goal. This can only be done in an environment where the child is supported by a loving adult.

Michael Jordan played junior varsity, not varsity, for his high school basketball team. Walt Disney was fired by a newspaper editor for not being creative enough. The Beatles were turned away from a record executive who told them that "guitar groups are on their way out." If you have had some failures, you must be on the way to finding the right path, and you are certainly in good company.

As a parent, it's important to let your children know you do not give up the first time you do not succeed. If you lose the ball at soccer, you do not stop playing. You start running even faster, more determined, to get the ball back. Children watch and learn how parents deal with disappointment.

What does not kill us, makes us stronger. Even individuals who became paraplegic as a result of spinal cord accidents quickly, within eight weeks, report more positive than negative emotions. Within a few years, they wind up only slightly less happy than individuals who are not paralyzed. Eighty-four percent of quadriplegics consider their life to be average or above average. [225]

It pays here to spend a few words on what is called 'posttraumatic growth.' After such trials as cancer, heart attack, military combat, natural disaster, or other seemingly terrible events, many studies show that positive growth follows. These benefits include personal strength, self-confidence, openness, better spirituality, compassion for others, better appreciation for, and greater intimacy in, social relationships.[226] These people can 'bounce forward,' and not 'bounce back', by seeing what positive they can make out from what terrible event has happened.

Mastery

With play, repeated thousands of times during practice, in an environment of connectedness, comes mastery of the skill. Few feelings in life are better than achieving mastery. "I can do it! I did it! Now I get it! Wow!" These are the cries of mastery. Once you feel such joy, you want to feel it again and again. Once you learn to ride a bike, you have learned a skill that can provide you with joy forever.

There are many other good examples of reaching mastery, such as when you first learned how to drive a car. Or, for me, when I saw my first medical books published. The feeling of mastery pushes the person to want to do more and more. You become self-motivated. You do not need external motivation, from parents, partner, colleagues, friends. The motivation comes from your own realization that working hard at something you are good at (your strength) has significant benefits, which matter to you directly. People like to do what they do well.

If you work your hardest, do a great job, and get a B, or even a C, that takes your self-motivation away. If this happens repeatedly, you may never recover, and go through life without ever trying hard again, without experiencing what striving your best can lead to. As an adult, that might happen in a non-meritocratic society, or with an ungrateful boss. Excessive criticism, or exceedingly high expectations, can be brought from the outside, most of the time, such as from parents, or teachers, or bosses. Or can even come from the inside, and we can be our worst enemies, not allowing ourselves the chance to try because we feel we can never achieve our dreams.

On the contrary, if you do not give the best of yourself and get an A anyway, that also will be counterproductive, as the lesson you'll interiorize will be that it does not pay to work hard, as one can get to the top without much sweat. The kid who is praised by parents no matter what as the best in the world will internalize the notion that dedication and working hard are not necessary in life. Once again, one of the keys to happiness, that is, working hard at a task that pushes yourself to the limit of your abilities and you deem important, gets lost, sometimes never to be recovered again.

Self-esteem is the result of mastery, not of just external praises. After you master a difficult task, your self-esteem naturally rises. I remember when I published my first paper in an important journal in my field, Obstetrics and Gynecology. At a large meeting, one of my colleagues showed the slide with the paper and my name, saying that was a big accomplishment. She made me realize it, and it gave me a sense of pride which has never left me.

After such successes, confidence, leadership skills, initiative, and enduring desire for hard work, ensue. You now want to work not because you feel you should, but because you want to, in order to experience that unbeatable feeling of mastery again.

So if you want to see a child succeed, make sure she experiencces mastery after practice and hard work. She will want to go back to these feeling. Make sure that your child understands that achieving something is not mastery. Mastery means that the achievement gives you the inner, personal feeling of realization. External praise has nothing to do with the feeling of mastery, which one can only feel inside herself. Continuous praise by parents cannot replace what the child needs to reach herself.

From mastery, comes also optimism. Optimism is the tendency to believe that there is always a realistic solution, that there is always hope, no matter how difficult things are or seem.

Some optimism is inherited genetically. I certainly was born an optimist, and I just cannot change into a pessimist. My being cannot even be forced to think that way. I imagine the same is true of some pessimists.

But childhood environment can certainly increase innate optimism. It can alleviate innate pessimism. And it can especially make an optimist of many people who were born, so to speak, neutral in attitude. How does one teach optimism? A parent and teacher should show the child how to see the positive side of things. How to interpret events in a more upbeat way. How to appreciate the silver lining. How not to concentrate on the negative. How not to let a defeat become the expected outcome of any future attempt.

To teach optimism, one needs to show how the child can be successful. At something, at anything. A child who gets to achieve a success, even a small accomplishment, learns to be optimistic. The bigger the success, the more the confidence, the more the optimism. Vice versa, a big early failure, noticed by dear ones, and seen publicly, can be devastating, and can lead to the making of a lifelong pessimist.

So the parent, in particular, needs to be aware of all the activities of her child, and put them in the correct positive contest. Awards and successes need to be correlated by the parent with the hard but fruitful work of the child. Failures need to be put in the right contest. Once again, connectedness with someone else to mentor the child through early life is essential.

One of the best references to teach a child how to be optimistic is Martin Seligman's 'Learned optimism.' Additionally, in 'The psychology of hope: you can get there from here," C. R. Snyder, states that the three elements to optimism in children are: 1. a goal; 2. will power, i.e. the energy one needs to achieve the goal; 3. *way*power, i.e. the inner feeling that you can find a way to reach your goal.

If you can raise your child to be optimistic, she'll have a higher chance of being happy as an adult. Optimism is one of the strongest predictors of adult happiness. And the beauty is, once you lean to think optimistically, that can stay with you a lifetime. Our younger son Pietro, as a 13 year old, scored as his top two strengths, out of twenty-five, Hope and Optimism, on the www.authentichappiness.com VIA Strength Survey for Children. He was born an optimist, but I hope he also strengthened it while growing up in a serene environment.

I'm happiest during and when I finish mastering something. For example, when I'm done writing a book. Or when I get to submit a scientific article. Or in the flow moments when I'm brainstorming over scientific data in the task to compose a cogent discussion part for the manuscript. This is best if I'm brainstorming the points with one of our fellows. I'm happy when I score a nice goal during a friendly soccer game at Starr garden in Philadelphia. I feel I accomplished something. I feel that I still 'got it.'

Recognition

Recognition is the feeling of being valued by others, especially others whose opinion the person respects. Many children can sense from an early age what other people want from them, and what they can do to gain the praise of others. When a child takes a first step, or learns to ride a bike, wild cheering occurs. It's important to give the child the right praise, for the right achievement. And it's important that they reach mastery and therefore deserve recognition for something they like, not others like. They should be valued and recognized for who they truly are, and their unique skills. They have found something they can do well.

Most adults can remember a teacher who inspired them to do excellent work, whose opinion the child really cared for, and who praised the child at the right moments, for the correct behaviors and achievements. Giving a child responsibility empowers them. Once you know that your task, your actions, matter to people who matter to you, then what you do becomes more uplifting to you.

This has another important consequence. You feel more closely connected to the people who have praised you. This recognition builds the bridge from mastery, back to connectedness.

Personally, becoming a doctor allowed me to get praises from my dad. It later allowed me to speak his language, the language of being an ob-gyn. When you learn to do something well, and someone else values this achievement of yours, you feel not only a sense of personal pride, but also a feeling of being connected with someone else, with the person you idolized and now is recognizing what you have done. Moreover, you feel a sense of connection with the whole organization, or profession, in this case, with all ob-gyn physicians.

Recognition is a natural validator that what we are doing has worth. This then motivates you to want to do more. Mikaly Csikszentmihalyi coined the term *autotelic*, which means internally motivated, from 'auto,' self, and 'telos,' goal. You play the piano because it pleases you, not to get a reward or external recognition. An autotelic person needs few material possessions and little entertainment, comfort, power, or fame, because so much of what he does is already rewarding in itself, for his own ego. The less one relies on external motivators and the more 'autotelic' one becomes, the happier one will be.

You need to make sure your child has moments during which he is enjoying who he is, and other people are enjoying who he is as well. So the experience is positive internally, and externally. The parent, or teacher, should guide the child towards activities which have a high chance to be associated with positive experiences. So that, at the end of a basketball game, you shout at your son "Good game Pietro!," the crowd is cheering for his winning shot with 2.9 seconds to go, and even he, Pietro, is beaming and convinced he played a good game. This actually happened in the spring of 2013. Once the child or young adult goes through this inner growth, she develops such qualities as self-esteem, and confidence. These virtues will need to be nurtured later, but usually last a lifetime, and are great contributors to happiness. The child will continue as an adult to participate, to reach up, to stretch forward.

Once you get recognized, you often get a stronger feeling of connectedness to the group. Let's say it is a team for which you scored, or you played a good game. Or you achieved a family goal. Or you won an award for which your school, or university, or co-workers also get recognition. This feeling of genuine connectedness to a larger group is the root of moral behavior.

When recognition is specific and deliberately delivered, it is more motivating than money.[227] When a leader allows a company worker to praise publically another employee, all three feel great about it. Of course, it is perhaps more important how you give recognition, in terms of attitude and tone of voice, than what exactly you say. And it's important to know that it takes about three positive comments, experiences, or expressions to fend off the languishing effects of one negative comment.[228]

For me, recognition is probably the best motivator. Recognition by the ones I love and/or admire is the main reason for my actions. My actions as a husband are motivated by my wife's recognition, my family's, and all my peers'. My actions as a father are motivated by my sons' recognition, my family's, and all my peers'. My actions at work are motivated by my peers' recognition, and by my family's. One of my strongest motivators, both personally and professionally, is being a good example to others.

One of the best kinds of recognition, for me, is reputation. If a person is known to be kind, usually other kind people will seek her out; and even non-nice people will try to be as nice as they can around a person with a reputation for being 'nice.' A person who is cruel usually finds that others are cruel back to him.[229] My personal and professional reputation are my proudest accomplishments, a lot more than any national or international award received.

There can be several possible problems with recognition. First, some children and then adults may learn to play a life-long game of people-pleasing, maybe for one of their parents, to the point that as adults they have no feeling of who they really are. Sometimes, even as adults, people cannot get rid of the sense of having to achieve at all cost to please the parent, forever.

Second, I have a sense that several of my high achieving colleagues, and myself included, have gotten used to recognition so much that we continue to seek more and more of it, without ever being able to truly relax a bit. But, on the other hand, balanced dedication has brought me sustained and deep happiness.

Third, if a child or later an adult needs recognition mainly as a mean to defeat others, the person can become a narcissist. This person has insatiable appetite for continuous praise. He is so concentrated on getting recognition, that he cannot give to others, cannot love, and therefore is alone, and unhappy.

The crucial differentiating factor between the narcissist's continuous need for praise and the normal person's healthy enjoyment of recognition for his own mastery is connectedness. The narcissist has never had, or lost along the way, connectedness to someone they admire, to a close family individual or friend.

I do know several narcissists. They may be excellent physicians who gave so much to the profession which gave them fame that they forgot to care for their own family. Or some who never even had time to create for themselves a true family, as they gave themselves no opportunity for connecting to others deeply, except for conferences or research projects. They could connect to a team, people with the same hobby, but they like themselves too much, and fly through life, even if constantly in front of the public eye, solo. Internally, they feel disconnected, alone.

Fourth, it is important to preserve the rush of enthusiasm that all children have, once the first successes arrive, once you get the first recognitions. It's a bit sad to reach the peak in life in terms of recognition and success when you are a teenager or at least less than 20-25 years old. It is important to maintain life-long enthusiasm, vision, and excitement, also discipline, patience, and determination.

Parent for happiness

You are most probably already an adult. You cannot change your childhood, and perhaps you found that some of your rearing was less than perfect while reading these pages. But still, assimilating the lessons about the childhood roots of adult happiness, you can become a better parent, a better uncle, a better babysitter, a better teacher.

As parents, we have a crucial role and an enormous responsibility towards our children. One we unfortunately should discuss more, be more aware of, and practice more. The most important thing we have to do as parents is love.

Parents should never forget how deeply children need to feel that they are safe and that they are loved. Curl-up in bed and give them a hug. Give them unconditional love. It is in giving love that we receive love. It is in giving that we receive.

A child should not have to win love. Contrary to secure attachment, a child who gets instead insecure attachment is in trouble for life, with permanent consequences.

Based again mainly on work done by Doctor Edward M. Hallowell,[230] we as parents can follow his detailed guide on activities we can encourage in our family to increase our children's level of happiness. Here is the list.

Talk to your children

It's really important to keep open communications with your kids. Give them advice. Last night, while the four of us together were out to dinner, the topic of spermatozoa came up. Possibly because wet dreams came up. Foster the spontaneity of discussing intimate issues. I drew on a napkin the female genital system, including uterus, tubes, and ovaries, and reviewed the menstrual cycle, when a woman is ovulating and therefore fertile, and how the egg and spermatozoon meet, as well as miscarriages and normal pregnancy. Our two sons were captivated, and Pietro kept the napkin for some class he had, to show his teacher.

Children absorb whatever we say. They are sponges for knowledge. A child may recall something a parent said weeks, months earlier. We notice this mostly when they recall something naughty, such as them remembering a ‘bad’ word. But they also remember us setting a good example for them. Whatever we do, they copy. Whatever we say, gets imprinted in what their own self will become.

Parents have a tremendous responsibility. Their words, the life they conduct in front of their children, sink in them deeper than what we acknowledge. So every day counts. We should take pleasure in enjoying this passing of good deeds on to our children.

Be interested, but not over interested, in what they do. Find ways to let them tell you. They usually like privacy. So be with them in a car ride, accompanying them or retrieving them from one of their activities. Be sure not to sound too nosey. First and foremost, be trustful, and do not let their secrets be known by anyone else. Not even your partner, if possible. The trust is between two people, the child and one parent, that’s it.

One of my best moments as a parent came one day when I was driving Andrea and Pietro to swimming. While I never drive to work, living five blocks away from the hospital, I do drive in the evenings and weekends taking them to their many activities. That day, the traffic was terrible, our usual 35 minutes ride to the pool was already 45 minutes, and we were not even halfway there.

I felt frustrated, stressed. I had run out of things to ask the kids. A few seconds of silence followed. Andrea broke the silence, saying, “Dad, I have something to tell you. Can you keep a secret?” He was 11 years old at the time. I suddenly became attentive, and excited. “Certainly Andrea, you can count on me.”

He went on to revel that he liked a girl in his 5th grade class, and that she did like him back. They were ‘going out.’ Since then, I do love it when traffic hits and prolongs the time I can spend with my sons in the car, talking about their thoughts, issues, problems, accomplishments, goals, loves.

Be understanding. Behave as you have open arms, and open ears, and whatever they want to tell, it's ok. As your children come to trust you, to know that you will not be harsh on them, and that they can share their inner thoughts openly with you, they will be more likely to tell you what they think. They will be more likely to open up about their insecurities. About a bully at school. About their first crushes.

Your role as a parent is to just be a shoulder they can lean on. An ear they can trust. A forum where they can serenely analyze verbally their thoughts, and their most inner feelings. It's a fantastic experience, for the child, but almost as much for the adult.

Spend time with your children

Apart from giving unconditional love, perhaps the second most important thing you can do for your children is spending quality time with them. Parent's presence at home is particularly important at critical times, such as morning, after school, dinner, bedtime. As we said above, children learn the most from following your example. Just you being around, and allowing him or her to understand your behavior and the values which drive it, is priceless. Parents should engage in activities with their child on a regular basis.

We have already reviewed so many activities that you can do with your children. Another important one is reading aloud to your children as long as they'll let you, when they are young. Or reading next to them, while they read their book and you read your book, providing a good model.

I like to play sports with my children. It promotes bonding. I recently ran a triathlon with Andrea, our older son. He had tremendous fun from the accomplishment, and I know he has internalized the importance of training leading to a good result, and of staying in shape during life at all ages.

Touch, hug, kiss, caress, massage your children. Wrestle, roll, and jump on the bed together. These are some of my favorite activities with them. I want to make them feel my affection in a physical way, not just in words, or acts of kindness. Kids are usually physical, and enjoy letting their energy all out.

Parents should state the concept of connectedness explicitly and directly to their children, "It is really important to us as a family that we create a feeling of togetherness, of connectedness." In our family, we have a sit down family dinner every night. There is no TV in our dining room. No electronics are allowed on the table. We share the experiences of our day. We open up our feelings regarding the main events. We plan the next activities.

We travel the world together as a family. We go to chess tournaments around the US together. We go out to dinner together. Just the four of us. Interestingly, it is not just the parents who should want this, but even more it is the children who need it. Pietro in particular, but also Andrea, want to go to dinner just the four of us. They are not shy, but like it less when Paola and I invite other friends.

Children who have previously described their relationship with parents as warm and close later experienced fewer than half as many serious illnesses as children who have characterized their relationship with parents as cold and distant.[231] Things that do impede connectedness include parents (or coaches, or teachers) ruling by intimidation.

Teach your kids the basic values of life

Some core values have stood the test of time. They are:[232]

- Wisdom; Knowledge
- Temperance; Self-control; Good manners
- Love; Altruism; Humanity
- Justice; Honesty; Sincerity
- Optimism; Seeking and emphasizing positive experiences; Suppressing or at least getting over bad memories

- Courage; Valor; Bravery; Hope; Dedication; Zest; Passion; Enthusiasm; Future-mindedness
- Forgiveness and Mercy
- Spirituality; Sense of purpose; Transcendence
- Playfulness and Humor

Many of these values include other strengths, so that wisdom includes curiosity, love of learning, judgment, critical thinking, open-mindedness, social intelligence, personal intelligence, emotional intelligence, and perspective. Love includes kindness, generosity, nurturance, gratitude, and the capacity to love but also the capacity to be loved. Temperance includes prudence, discretion, caution, humility and modesty, to be polite, interpersonal skills, to let a woman go first, to wait your turn, to not cut in front of people, to listen to others, and to share.

Obviously several of these virtues overlap. These strengths are moral traits. They should be distinguished from talents, such as physical beauty, speed in running, or perfect pitch, which are non-moral.

These strengths are the same in all major religions, and philosophy. The Ancient Egyptians, the Old Testament, The Talmud, Aristotle, Plato, Confucius, Buddha, the Koran, all are based on these same values. They have been summed up in these values: 1. Golden rule of reciprocity – do to others what you wish was done to you; 2. Non-violence and respect for life; 3. Justice and solidarity; 4. Honesty and tolerance; 5. Mutual esteem and partnership.[233]

The most important part of these values and strengths is that they can be acquired. Talents are hard to come by. But with dedication and exercise, the strengths above can be acquired and made a daily spontaneous routine by almost anyone.

Responsibility to contribute

Children need to be taught since very young that it is better to give, than to receive. In a family, kids should begin to appreciate that they do not just take, but also give and contribute. Children who do chores around the house develop a can-do, want-to-do attitude. They are industrious.

There is something magic about doing something for others, which makes us feel good. I remember well when, about 14 years old, I was sent by my parents to buy pizza, about three blocks from the house. Outside it was cold and drizzly, and at first I felt I was being exploited. But I never forgot the feeling of accomplishment when I realized I could do it, and I later got them positive emotions with warm delicious pizza. Now I just wanted to get another such chore, to experience again the same sense of achievement, of success. To feel like I would get in deeper in their hearts.

Feeling others owe you is wonderful. Not because you want them to pay you back, but just because of the feeling that someone you love recognizes you as a good person. Kids who understand this connection between doing a chore and positive personal feelings are more likely, later in life, to get a paid job outside the house. Parents should have high expectation of school performance, but not pretend their kids absolutely get into Harvard.

This sounds a bit Calvinistic. Obviously one can exaggerate on the other extreme. A kid may begin to do his bed, but should not do every bed in the house. If the young adult is studying productively in school, they should not work hard also outside of school. But a little bit of work is therapeutic, at any age, even in the very young and very old.

Also, teach your kids that a high-achieving student can also hang out with friends and play. One does not have to sell his soul, in order to excel. My motto: Work hard, play hard.

The individual's own self

Make sure your children cultivate what is special in them. Virtually every advance in human history came from people who were brave enough to allow themself to think differently, to ignore at times common beliefs, and to not be afraid to 'sing outside the choir.'

These exceptional persons acted against the mob, were maybe even vilified, disbelieved, initially. Think Semmelweis, Einstein, Galileo, Leonardo. As my mother told me over and over again, kids need to be incentivized to have a mind of their own, to think with their own head. Humans should always search for the truth, but be very wary of constantly keeping the company of those who claim to have found it. It's the doubters, who go out to test new hypotheses, who will advance the world.

Family traditions

Preserve, continue, or invent, family traditions. I grew up with a lot of old traditions, in particular thanks to my father. He bought back the house where he was born, in an 800-people village called Sant'Apollinare. There we make wine together as a family, as many generations of Berghella's have done. We sing at the top of our lungs 'Tu scendi dalle stelle' during the night of the 24th of December. My brother Michele has told me bluntly that Christmas does not arrive for them unless I'm in Abruzzo, the region in Italy where I'm from and all my relatives live, except for my wife and children.

I myself have continued a lot of these traditions, such as the singing, and have taken my son Andrea to watch the grape harvest ('la vendemmia'). I named Andrea after my father's name. For at least the last seven generations, Andrea and Vincenzo have been the two first names which have alternated for the first sons of the new generation.

Involve the kids in creating, and then maintaining, new

traditions of their own. For example, we eat at McDonalds or Kentucky Fried Chicken only during road trips. Do your traditions over, and over, and over again, year after year. Your kids will love it.

A sense of the past

It's important for children to hear the history of their family. I love taking Andrea and Pietro to the family chapel in Sant'Apollinare's cemetery. Seeing Vincenzo Berghella (my grandfather's name), Andrea Berghella (my great-grandfather's name) written on the tombs brings chills in my body every time, and I think now it does for my sons. I have put together a Berghella family pedigree going back several generations, and of course I have also added to it my wife Paola Luzi's family lineage, which is actually longer, more accurate, and more distinguished.

My father is at his best, I feel, when he recounts what happened to the Berghella family during World War II. For example, the story of when a German bomb hit their house, came through the roof, and down the stairs, but, miraculously, did not explode. Or the account of when the Germans invaded our region, and my dad, his parents, and his brother, had to live in a cave. Or the anecdote of when his father, Vincenzo Berghella, hid lots of money in a stable, but then, at the end of the war, he went back to find that the stable had burned.

The oral history of the family is the most gripping history a child ever learns. It is the history she is most likely to remember as an adult. It is the history which most will guide her actions and choices in later life.

For me, my connection with my father has given greater meaning to my professional successes as an obstetrician, as he really understands them, having had the same profession. Regarding my mother, she wanted me to be a diplomat like her uncle, and when I get praises for my team-building skills and mediation qualities they are more meaningful to me because of my connection with her.

I am warmed by fires that some of my ancestors lighted, and that keep on burning inside myself. I receive tremendous inner satisfaction from keeping these fires burning ever bigger, hoping that my larger group, the members of my family, enjoy my successes a bit as their own.

Friends

Friends matter. They are a social capital. A life asset. Like money in the bank. If you have good, true friends, you have a much better chance of being happy. Not only. You even have a better chance of being healthy. The child needs to be loyal to his friends. To never bully or embarrass them.

You gain friends by making them feel included. When I was introduced to my new 5th grade class in a new town, one of the kids volunteered to have me as his desk mate. Antonello ended up being one of the two best men at my wedding. Basically, by treating others the way you would like to be treated, you gain friends.

Parents need to show their children how they cherish their friends, how they try to keep in touch, remember their birthdays, help them when in need, being available for their friend's venting. Just like when choosing a partner, choosing a life-long friend involves finding out her values, which, of course, derive from her parents. So if you like someone's parents, it is very likely you'll like them, too.

The world of the spirit

Parents do not need to be overly religious to be helpful to their children. But it has been shown that thanking God, or whatever higher being we might believe in, for our good fortunes (everyone has some) is helpful, and contributes to a feeling of happiness.

This can be saying prayers before bedtime. Or saying grace before meals. Or just learning to talk to God in special moments, such as when gazing out from the rim of the Grand Canyon. Even in difficult moments, meditating can be very helpful.

Learning, ideas and information

Praise learning. The learning done at home, the learning done at school, and the learning we can receive in every moment of our life. Continue to study. Get a degree as an adult parent, showing how much enjoyment you get from the experience, and the child will internalize how important learning is in reaching happiness. Encourage your children to always ask, 'Why?' Make them lifelong learners.

Expose them to everything. To every possible topic, such as nature, science, animals, the world of beauty and the arts. Show them how they can get more information for themselves, without you forcing excessive passive information on them. Make them active investigators of what they are interested in.

Avoid expecting too much, or expecting they live the life YOU want for them

The childhood roots of unhappiness are parents who expect more from a child than the child can deliver. Also, parents who set up goals and standards the child can never meet. To expect too much is a curse for a child. 'Do your best' is instead advice that instills the right amount of pressure.

One of the biggest parental mistakes is to put too much emphasis on a certain goal. So if the child does not get into Harvard, get the Nobel price, or win at the Olympics, then they are a failure, and happiness is precluded. Do not tie your love for your child to your child meeting these expectations.

Many Harvard graduates are unhappy, having achieved their parent's dream, but not theirs. As many as eighty percent of Harvard students suffer from depression during the school year.[234] One should play his/her own game. Sometimes it takes a midlife crisis to realize it.

As Edward M Hallowell said, "What determines success and happiness in life is, of course, not the quality of the college to which the person goes, but the quality of the person who goes to college."[235] I love this phrase, and I've repeated it to my sons.

The young adult's imagination, ambition, perseverance, maturity, discipline, and ability are what leads to success, not the college. A great kid will make the most of a mediocre college, while an average Joe may squander the opportunities given by exceptional teachers at top colleges. I do know my share of unhappy Harvard graduates.

As Shawn Achor said, "If my calculations are correct, 99% of Harvard students do not graduate in the top 1%."[236] This fact often destroys the confidence of persons whose expectations have been for perfection, not happiness; perfection is the enemy of good, in certain cases. Harvard undergraduates have on average less than one romantic relationship and 0.5 sexual partners over the four years of college. [237] They have very little social support, which is the number one key to happiness. I know many superb adults who went to school at places I never heard of.

The main dangers of pretending Harvard or nothing else for your child are two. First, if she fail to get into Harvard, she is a failure (even if you get into Princeton or Yale). Second, having as the sole goal enrolling at an Ivy League college prevents the talented youth from developing her own true best self, from cultivating her own strengths.

It's ok for parents to hold a child responsible. It is ok to put a bit of pressure on the child. It is ok to demand return on investment. I'm ok with, "I came over here from Poland, and sacrificed my whole life without even an education, to give you a chance at an education and at a better life."

But let's not exaggerate; I resented a bit when my father used to say that he worked because of us children; even if it worked in motivating us. I don't think my father worked so hard just to put bread on the table, and to show us what a good example he was. He liked what he did, felt responsible for his patients and for his team of colleagues, and I'm sure he would have worked just as hard if he were single with no kids. He chose voluntarily to have children.

Of course, not only parents have to believe in their children. Another key role is that of teachers. I think the following scientific study makes the point here perfectly. A team of researchers performed intelligence tests on elementary students. Then they told the teachers that they had identified certain students, let's say Sarah, Joe, and Sally, as the superstars. The teachers were told not to reveal the results to the students, and to treat all students equally, as they would be watched to do so.

At the end of the year, Sarah, Joe, and Sally, did best on objective tests. The fact was, these three had scored average on the initial test. Their only advantage was that their teachers *believed* they were better, even if they were not. These nonverbal messages by the teachers were noticed somewhat subconsciously by the students, who then performed better.[238] This phenomenon is called the Pygmalion effect. Our belief in the other person's ability brings their potential to reality.

Benefits of happiness

I would hope that by now you are getting convinced of the importance of being happy. But, in fact, there is a ton of scientific data to answer the question, 'Why be happy?'[239] More scientific evidence and references on the dozen of personal benefits of being happy are available in the World Happiness Report 2013.[240]

Compared to less happy peers, happier people enjoy several benefits.[241,242,243]

- Mood, behavior, sociability, and productivity, organization, and income
  - *More creative*. Happier people tend to have more flexibility and ingenuity in their thinking. Doctors put in a positive mood (given a candy!) make an accurate diagnosis 19% faster than controls. Optimistic sales people outsell their pessimistic counterparts by 56%.[244]
  - *Better thinkers*. Positive emotions flood our brains with dopamine and serotonin. These chemicals make us feel good, but also make learning centers in our brain work better, helping organize information more efficiently, keeping that information in the brain longer, and retrieving it faster later on.[245]
  - *Better test takers*. Some students were told to think about the happiest day of their life before taking a standardized math test. They scored better than controls.[246]
  - *Better leaders and negotiators*. People who expressed more positive emotions during business deals did so more efficiently and successfully than those who were neutral or negative.[247] Managers who provide frequent recognition and encouragement lead teams who perform 31% better than teams led by less optimistic, positive, and happy managers.[248] A single negative

individual at work can worsen the morale for the entire group.[249]

- *More sociable*. Being happy fosters more and higher quality interactions and relationships.[250] People want to be with a happy person, not with an unhappy person. When we are with a positive individual, we tend to be more positive, too. Happy people are in general better liked by others. Therefore, happier people are more likely to get married, and also to stay married. They have a richer network of friends, and therefore a lot more social support. For example, girls who looked sincerely happy on the photos on their college yearbook were more likely to get married by age 27, and more likely to have satisfying marriages by age 52.[251] Happier people tend to be more popular, and likeable. So they make more and closer friends. And making better friends, in return, makes them happier. Happy people also are better colleagues, neighbors, and citizens.[252]
- *More cooperative and collaborative*.[253]
- *Spend less and save more*.[254]
- *More pro-social behavior: more charitable; donate more money, time, and blood;*[255] *volunteer more.*[256] When people are in a good mood, they tend to help others. In turn, helping others fosters good mood. This is an effective catch-22 situation, powerfully leading to very high happiness levels.
- *More resilient when faced with challenges.*
- *Able to exercise self-control.* For example by delaying gratification with the aim of achieving larger benefits in the future.[257] Happier individuals are better able to pursue long-term goals.[258]
- *Higher productivity.* Both at work and at home. Unhappy employees take an extra 15 sick days a year.[259]

- *Greater achievements.* They rated higher by supervisors.[260]
- *More successful.* Many believe that success brings happiness. As we said before, this is true, as achievement and recognition bring happiness. But, in addition, *being happy also fuels success*. It is often not true that success comes first, and happiness second. In fact, it is more causative that happiness is first, then followed as a consequence by success. Happiness is the precursor of success. All the benefits of being happy listed so far make us more effective and prosperous. This is a huge paradigm shift. Before Copernicus and 1543, we used to think that the sun orbited around the earth. Before recently, we used to think that happiness orbited around success. In fact, like the sun and the earth, the contrary is true. Happiness is the center, like the sun, and success revolves around it.[261] Happiness leads to success in every domain of our lives, such as marriage, health, friendship, community service, creativity, our work, and career.[262]
- *Get re-employed faster and more often.*[263]
- *Get promoted more often. Earn more money.* A study has shown, for example, that happier college freshman end up having higher salaries 16 years later compared to their less happy but otherwise similar peers.[264] Another study measured positive emotions in employees, and then eighteen months later showed that the happier employers ended up receiving better evaluations and higher pay later on.[265] Happiness is associated with higher income.[266] Happiness also predicts future income.[267]

- Health and longevity
  - *Better sight.* In one study, people were primed with either positive or negative emotions. Then they looked at pictures. Those with the better mood saw everything,

more details of the background, and had an expanded peripheral line of vision.[268] This benefit obviously helps to comprehend and process things better all day long, in any activity.

- *Improved cardiovascular and endocrine health.*[269] Positive affect is associated with lower risk of heart disease - especially coronary artery disease - and stroke.[270] Positive feelings are associated with lower body fat, lower blood pressure, and lower body mass index.[271]
- *Improvement in immune system.* Happiness levels were measured in volunteers, who were then injected with the cold virus. A week later, the happier individuals had fought off the virus more efficiently, and objective measurements by doctors on cold signs and symptoms in these happier-to-begin-with people were better than less happy controls.[272]
- *Reduced inflammation.*[273]
- *Less stress and anxiety.* A group of people was asked to give a public speech (one of the situations deemed most stressful by humans) which would be videotaped and judged. They were first assigned randomly to watch happy, neutral, or sad videos. The ones who watched the video which induced feelings of joy and contentment and were so primed with positive feelings, experienced a faster recovery from the stress of giving the videotaped public speech.[274]
- *Eat better diet, healthier foods such as fruits and vegetables; exercise more.*[275] You feel better. You are more energetic.
- *Take less health risks.* Happier people use seat-belts more often while driving, and are involved in less car accidents.[276]
- *Lower suicide rates.*[277]

- *Have healthier pregnancies*. Happier women miscarry pregnancy less, have less preterm births, and have more babies with an healthy weight.[278]
- *Quicker recovery from disease*.[279]
- *Longer life*. A group of nuns was asked to write about their thoughts and emotions in their diaries while in their 20's. Five decades later, the nuns with the diaries with more joyful content were found to have lived nearly 10 years longer than nuns with neutral or negative content. By age 85, 90% of the happiest quartile, and 34% of the lowest quartile, were still alive.[280,281] Happiness lowers the risk of mortality in both healthy and diseased individuals.[282] People with less life stress have longer telomeres (the ends protecting our DNA). This may be one of the many mechanisms for increased longevity.[283] It is not a long life which makes us happy. We have a longer life because we were happier to begin with.

This is the 'Happiness advantage.'[284] Even the smallest shots of positivity can give someone a serious competitive edge. As one can see, some of these benefits are related, and clearly feed on one another. Being more sociable leads to better collaboration, and team work has been shown to lead to better work, which then leads to praise, which leads to more satisfaction, which is associated with happiness.[285]

With my leader's hat, these concepts remind me of the famous concept publicized by Jack Welsh, the iconic former CEO of General Electric: "Hire for attitude, train for skill." Success comes when one grabs life and lives it to the fullest. It's an attitude, not a skill. The attitude leads to the skill.

Your happiness depends on you

"Our life is the creation of our mind"

Buddha[286]

Is it possible to train the mind just as the body? And train the mind to be happy? Absolutely. Happiness is something you choose. You can indeed learn to change your thinking. We can control our own future. This belief that we can is one of the biggest drivers to happiness and success.

The mental construction of our daily activities, more than the activity itself, defines our reality.[287] As we have seen above, our brain can be changed. Another example which we have not mentioned yet is the placebo effect. If we believe a drug is going to work, it often will, even if it is not even a drug which has effects.

In another experiment, hotel cleaning staff employees were told that their work was associated with calorie burned, exercise, and health benefits, while some controls were not. The cleaning personnel primed to think of their work as exercise lost more weight, and had even lower cholesterol levels. These individuals had not done any more work, nor had they exercised any more than the controls. The only difference was in how their brains had conceived of the work they did.[288]

The experience of happiness changes us and changes the world. Varied states of well-being influence gene expression by epigenetics.[289] Happiness has persisted in evolution as a beneficial trait, as it helps survival, reproduction, and social, personal, and professional success.[290]

You need to take control of your life. Employees who feel high levels of control at the office are better at their job, have more satisfaction in their work and family life, with less stress, work-family conflict, and job turnover.[291] These people have an internal, not external, 'locus of control' on their lives. When elderly nursing home residents were given more control over their lives, such as being in charge of their own plants, their happiness levels improved, and their mortality dropped in half![292]

To pursue happiness, one has to exercise to achieve it. Happiness does not come to you without a concerted effort to *create* it for yourself.[293] If you want to do well at a sport, you practice hard. Michael Jordan for basketball, Jackie Joyner-Kersee for track and field, Roger Federer for tennis, Lionel Messi for soccer, are just the most obvious examples of complete dedication to a goal, excellence in their respective sport. Since the time they were young teenagers, they spent countless hours practicing.

While the vast majority of us never achieve the level of mastery of world-famous athletes, or world-famous anything, we do often become experts in something we like, such as repairing clothes, electronics, gardening, or shopping. We should, also, concentrate our efforts into becoming experts at how to become happy.

Happiness is also convincing ourselves that we like to do what we have to do. I do this all the time. Examples are brushing teeth, flossing, going to work, etc. "Nothing is miserable unless you think it so: and on the other hand, nothing brings happiness unless you are content with it."[294]

Happiness is not about lying to ourselves, or turning a blind eye to the negative. A happy person is not dumb. Happiness is adjusting our brain so that we can see ways to rise above our baseline genetic happiness level.[295]

Shawn Achor makes the fulcrum and lever comparison. Some of us have the fulcrum already positioned so that our lever is long, and we can generate a lot of power (positivity). Some of us have the fulcrum positioned so that our lever is short, and we can generate little power (negativity). For most of us, the fulcrum is in some mid-position.

All of us, though, can try to move the fulcrum in a more optimal position, to get a longer lever, and more happiness.[296] 'Reality' is whatever our own brain understands of the world's circumstances. It is based on what we observe, and how we 'feel' it, interpret it. We can change this prospective, about anything, at any moment. A move to a more positive interpretation of things can improve our well-being.

Consider how much time you already devote to your physical appearance, i.e. going to the gym, exercising, or just buying clothes or make-up. If you desire happiness, you should give an even extra effort into activities which have been proven scientifically to increase your happiness.

So, in summary, do not leave happiness to chance alone. Happy people do not sit around waiting for happiness to come to them. They make things happen. They actively pursue their goals. They seek companionship and social interactions. They control their thoughts and feelings towards looking at the glass-half-full view of their opportunities in life.[297]

Be connected with your peers, with your clients, and with your patients if you are a health care worker. Be caring and compassionate with them. Social ties are an extremely reliable indicator of happiness. Human relationships and connections of all kinds contribute more to happiness than anything else. Find mentors. Be part of a team. People are the most important thing.

Do what you like to do. Play to your strengths. Dream big. Find engagement and meaning in your calling. Be positive. Hold the light so people not only can see you, but can also follow your lead to health and happiness. You can make a huge difference in any person you come in contact with.

Happiness practice exercises

Just as it takes over 10,000 hours to master basketball, or piano, repeated practice is necessary to master happiness. In fact, Confucius compared moral development to playing music, both needing many years of practice.[298] Aristotle used a similar metaphor, "Men become builders by building houses, and harpists by playing harp. Similarly, we grow just by the practice of just actions, ..."[299]

I will now review some easy exercises, and general advice, which are scientifically proven to improve your happiness level.[300] We are all a bit different, so that you should pick the happiness strategies below which suit you best. Happiness is an attitude, and needs to be cultivated with great effort, and attention to detail. Set small, moderately difficult, manageable goals.

1. *By reading this book*, you clearly have demonstrated you do have the right attitude to at least aim to improve your happiness level. Practice what you have underlined as pertinent to you in these pages. If you have not done any underling or taken notes, please go back and extract from these pages what most seems to apply to you, and make it your own exercise.
2. *Strive to be more positive* even in daily, routine, seeming futile interactions. Smiling produces neurochemicals which actually do make us happy. This is sometimes called the facial feedback hypothesis, and suggests to 'fake it until you make it.' Change your facial expression to a positive one, and you will feel beneficial emotional change.[301]

   Greeting other people in a positive manner not only helps you, but it helps others, too. When people ask me how I'm doing, over 95% of the times I reply, "Excellent." Not only does it remind me of the good things I have going for myself. It also gives a boost to my proxy to look on her bright side. So say, "Excellent" when asked, "How are you?"

and you will feel excellent having also improved someone else's life.

A positive attitude is contagious. Not only do we affect positively the person we are directly interacting with. The influence appears to extend to people within three degrees. And there are nearly 1,000 people within three degrees of most of us. So by being positive, at any time, we improve the lives of a 1,000 people around us![302] Like a single butterfly flapping its wings once can cause a hurricane halfway around the world, so can we. And that hurricane is happiness!

This effect on others is sometimes called the mirror effect. When we are pricked by a needle, neurons send pain messages to the brain. Later, when we see someone else receive a needle prick, the same neurons light up in us. When a boss walks in a room in a bad mood, most other people's mood worsens.[303]

When we are in a positive mood, people like us better, and friendship, love, and partnerships are more likely to be successful. When we are positive, we are more creative, tolerant, expansive. We are open to new ideas and new experiences.[304] Studies have shown that a positive emotion, such as getting a smile, a candy, watching a comedy or cartoon, hearing a compliment, predispose us to do better with the next task at hand. The more genuinely expressive someone is, the more the positive influence towards happiness for others spreads.[305]

We can actually see the same object, or the same situation, differently than others. Two shoe salesmen were sent to Africa to assess the market there in the early 1990's. One wired back to his boss, "Situation hopeless. They do not have any shoes." The other wrote, "Glorious opportunity! They do not have any shoes yet!"[306] Consider that both these assessments are completely hypothetical. We actually have the power in any situation to consciously select a counterfact that makes us feel fortunate, rather than helpless.

As always, use moderation and balance, as forced optimism does not mean ignoring reality.

3. *Be open to accept the positive boost you get when people are positive towards you.* When people say "Count your blessings," "Look on the bright side," "Smile," "Be happy," they are helping us. These are important to us, they are not just meaningless conversation.[307] Make sure you get the boost they are supposed to provide. The happier people are around you, the happier you will become. In a theater full of laughing people, you'll laugh more; this is also why television sitcoms have a laugh track.[308]
4. *Write done at least three good things that happened to you every day.* University of Pennsylvania professor Martin Seligman proved the effectiveness of this exercise with a scientific experiment.[309] Writing, for example, "Rosalind called to say hello," "I read a chapter of a book my therapist recommended," and "The sun finally came up today," were associated, within 15 days, with 94% of the persons doing this exercise experiencing relief, and their depression going from severe to mild or moderate. [310] When these positive experiences are then recalled, for example at least twice a week by transporting our mental attention to them, one is better able to find a new prospective and self-insight into current issues, and to enjoy her present life.[311]
5. *Celebrate good news.* Congratulate people, especially family and friends, on their accomplishments. Do not be shy about sharing with them your own little successes. Do not shy away from pride. Imagine how happy it will make you feel to share your good news, and enjoy the moment you get the smile of gratification and recognition back from your loved ones.[312]
6. *Devote a great amount of time and effort into cultivating your relationship with family and friends.* Invest in social connections.
7. *Express your gratitude to others* - including God, if you like - warmly, sincerely, and often. Send thank you notes. Write

down the names of the people who had the most positive influence on your personal, and also on your professional life. Write them a nice note; make an appointment with them; and read it to them, giving them a copy to keep.

8. *Be helpful to others*, including coworkers, or strangers who cross your path during your day. Perform acts of kindness and generosity. Acts of altruisms, such as giving to friends or to strangers, decrease stress and strongly contribute to enhanced mental health.[313,314] Performing five acts of kindness a day is associated with increases in happiness, which last for many subsequent days, even after the exercise has been over a while.[315]

   For example, I always let others get in first, and get out first, at doors and elevators. Some like to pay the toll for the car beyond. This has been shown to then let the lucky stranger perform act of kindness to others in return. Be a Good Samaritan. Do to others what you would like would be done to you. Live by the principle of reciprocity.

9. *Practice optimism* when imaging your future. Try to look at the bright side of all events. Find the silver lining. Notice more what's right, and less what's wrong. Believe that your goal can be accomplished. This again may be different for different people. Some may be better at small goals, as in "My bus will be on time today." Some will be able to stretch this exercise to bigger hopes, such as "I'll get the job." All that is required to be an optimist is to have a goal and to practice it.

   The world can be seen as a horrible, cruel place, or as a wonderful place of opportunities. You have a choice of how to evaluate it. Optimistic people just choose, on their own will, the happiness path. They are not unrealistic. In fact, research shows that optimists are more vigilant of risks and threats,[316] but they are also more aware that positive outcomes are dependent on their efforts.

   Optimistic thoughts can be self-fulfilling. If you think

you can achieve the goal, you'll have a much higher chance of realizing it. Optimistic people are less likely to give up, and more likely instead to take the initiative and be persistent towards the aim.[317] Make yourself be excited about every moment you go through in life. It will have two great effects: more happiness for you, and more for those around you.

In failure, try to focus on external reasons, rather that routinely on internal causes. So think, "The weather was not good, that's why few people came to my stand today," rather than "I'm terrible at making a pretty stand, and as a small business man," remaining though in reality, and not always excusing yourself.

Do identify the causes for failure to achieve your goal, so to be able to reinterpret the situation. For kids, for example, if a boy does not return a text message, it does not mean always "He hates me." What is the evidence for this? We must refocus our brain to think that it is quite possible that "He's is too busy today."[318]

Thinking about your best possible self has been proven to enhance mood.[319] In fact, writing about your goals and your life is even better than just thinking about them. The systematic, structured review you do on paper allows you to learn about yourself, your priorities and your most important values, and to find meaning in your life experiences.[320] Writing often clarifies what is most important to us, and what we want to, and can, achieve. William Faulkner reportedly once said, "I never know what I think about something until I read what I've written on it."[321]

10. *Savor life pleasures*

Eating a meal, taking a shower. Writing. The sweetness of a ripe mango. The aroma of a bakery. The warmth of the sun. Even walking to the subway. Taking a bike ride to work. Enjoy the moment that you are doing something absorbing (e.g. writing a paper for me), and also the moment that you get the task accomplished. Share these with your loved ones.

Enjoy all beauty and excellence around you. The sights. The sounds. The experiences. You might get a positive emotion from a ray of sunshine. From a concerto. From seeing a friend. Be aware of the happiness all things around you do bring.

Robert Brault said it well, "Enjoy the little things, for one day you may look back and realize they were the big things."

11. *Live in the present moment.*

This New Yorker cartoon says it all: sometimes we just do not take the time to enjoy what we are doing at the very moment, always wishing to be somewhere else, doing something else. I often think, when I see a nice boat, that I envy those on the yacht, but those on the yacht probably envy my freedom on land. I've taught myself to understand this, and therefore to be happy on land, or, when I'm on it, rarely, on a boat.

During life, one is mostly thinking about the future as

the reward, and not about the present as the reward. For example, parents tell their children to be good, so they can become later honest adults. Teachers incentivize their students to study hard, so to get into better colleges, and then better jobs as adults. Bosses push their employers to work hard, with the goal of a future raise or promotion. And then, when one retires, there seems to be not much future, health problems arise, and even retirement is often not enjoyed. We rarely seem to live and enjoy the present moment. We should enjoy what we do now for what it is worth, for its 'flow' value.

Clearly, one can savor the *past* by savoring it in the *present*. This is particularly true of older individuals, as it has been shown that the more time they spend reminiscing, the more positive affect and higher morale they report.[322] Even for other people, carrying and looking occasionally at an album of family and friends photographed during happy activities, can be associated with little bursts of happiness.[323] Try to focus on the past positive experiences, not on the negative ones.

One can also savor the *future* by anticipating in the *present* upcoming events (e.g. a trip, a visit with loved ones). In fact, joyful anticipation, the looking forward to desired activities, is associated with optimism and positive emotions. This is a strong typical feature of my character. These are activities clearly associated with happiness.

But one has to, probably most of the time, enjoy and live the present. Being able to not only be in flow, but also to step aside it after, and savoring it, is associated with several benefits, including more self-confidence and gratification, and less hopelessness and neurosis.[324] While listening to music, or getting a massage, close your eyes, and stay absorbed in the present, letting your mind go.

Even in traffic, a situation usually associated with unhappiness, people can find a brighter side, and even flow.

They can listen to the news on the radio. They can enjoy music, and think in meditation. They can talk to friends or family, one of the activities which give the most well-being. They can listen to a book being read, or to a lecture on something they are interested in.

12. *Search for activities which cause you to be in flow.* These are challenging tasks that stretch your skills and expertise, that you can completely engross yourself in, and that you can succeed in, master, to then get internal rewards and external recognition. Flow is inherently pleasurable and fulfilling, and gives a natural high.

Identify these talent areas. Then try to spend as much time in them as you can. Direct your attention fully to the task at hand. This can be music, or math, or softball. As you get better at them, increase the level of skill, play with better players, find more difficult problems. We should like to escalate our goals, enjoying the intensity of the effort along the way, without worrying too much about the ultimate goal, which will come because of our industry and determination anyway.

Be open to new experiences, and to life-long learning. Just like a child does. While at work, try to spend more time in high-challenge, high-skill situations, so situations that foster flow.[325] People who think that happiness is just coasting by, and doing the minimum necessary, choosing the easy tasks, have it all wrong.

Time your happiness activities well. I time my bike rides to when it's most pleasantly warm and sunny outside, which is my preference. I write mostly in the morning, when my brain is best suited to.

Not to fall into adaptation, also try to change slightly your favorite activities. I always have a new study project. A new book to write. A slightly different path to bike ride. At the same time, though, try to develop a habit of doing activities which you know bring happiness.

An average employee gets interrupted every 11 minutes, losing concentration and flow. It takes at least 8 minutes to regain concentration and flow.[326] Many check emails 5-times an hour, and the average employee spends 107 minutes on email a day.[327] Avoid these pitfalls.

13. *Play to your strengths.* You will get more happiness rewards from using your best skills, your signature strengths. Pick one of your strengths (by taking the test online at www.authentichappiness.com) and use it in a new way for a week, and you will be significantly happier and less depressed than controls.[328] See Appendix A for a list of strengths, and how I did!

14. *Believe in yourself.* The more one believes in her ability to succeed, the more likely it is that it will happen. Success almost becomes a self-fulfilling prophecy. Accountants who believed at the outset that they could accomplish their goals, had ten months later the best job performance. Belief in their own ability was a stronger predictor than their actual level or training or skill.[329]

When asked before a test to disclose their race, African Americans perform worse on standardized tests, compared to when they are not asked to do so. On the same standardized test, blacks performed worse than whites before the election of Barack Obama to President of the United States, but similar to whites, filling the gap, when they took the same test after the election.[330] One has to believe in herself or himself to succeed.

So when faced with a difficult task and challenge, focus on all the reasons you will succeed, on the skills you have, on your willingness to do the tasks necessary to get to the goal, on similar situations in which you did well in the past. And also, believe you can improve. Seventh-grade students who believed they could improve, compared to those who thought they could not, improved their GPA when in 9th grade.[331]

When we believe there will be a positive payoff for our efforts, we work harder instead of giving up.

15. *Improve your physical surroundings*. Pictures of loved ones in your home and work give a hit of positive emotions every time we glance at them. Watch less TV, and especially less violent media: this makes us happier.[332] Spend at least 20 minutes outside when the weather is good: it increases positive mood, broadens thinking, and improves working memory.[333]

16. *Make physical exercise a habit* at least every other day, if not daily. Exercise releases pleasure-inducing chemicals called endorphins. Exercise improves motivation, helps us get in flow, and get feelings of mastery. Depressed patients were assigned to antidepressant medications, exercise for 45 minutes three times a week, of a combination of the two, for 4 months. Exercise and medication were equally effective!

    Additionally, six more months later during which no intervention was suggested, the relapse rate was 38% in the medication-only group, 31% in the combination group, and only 9% in the exercise-only group, showing that physical activity is not only a powerful mood lifter, but also a long-lasting one.[334]

17. *Meditate*. Monks who spend time meditating actually physically grow their left prefrontal cortex, which is the part of the brain where happiness is, the part of the brain most responsible for our feelings of well-being.[335] Meditation also increases self-esteem, empathy, trust, and memory, as well as lowers stress, and improves the immune system.[336]

18. *Find something to look forward to*. The most enjoyable part of an activity is often the anticipation. People who thought about watching their favorite movie actually raised their endorphin levels by 27%![337] For me, thinking about a future book, article, play with my kids, quality time with my wife, one-on-one deep conversations with a close friend, are

activities which generate positive emotions even before they happen, just anticipating them.

19. *Stay deeply committed to your lifelong goals* and ambitions.
20. *Cope with challenges with poise and strength.* Develop strategies for coping. Analyze unpleasant events to cast them in a better light. Learn to forgive.
21. *Avoid overthinking and social comparison.* A bronze Olympic medalist is happier than a silver medalist. The bronze is happy because she did better that all the ones who did not get any medal, and is relieved that instead she got a medal. The silver is disappointed that she was so close to win it all, to get gold, and feels like she could have, should have, done better. Low expectations are a good strategy; don't expect to win, it will be a nice surprise; still do everything you can to win. Underpromise (yourself, as well as others), and overdeliver.

These sorts of training have been scientifically proven to be associated with a significant improvement in the level of happiness.[338] Each of these activities gives us a boost of positive emotions if performed habitually over time. They can permanently raise our happiness baseline, which, as we said, can indeed be raised.

As each of us has values, interests, strengths, and weakness, which are all a bit different, it's of great importance to know them to be able to choose our personal best path to happiness. The Person-Activity fit diagnostic test of Sonja Lyubomirsky, for example, helps find the activities which best fit you. You can do it at http://thehowofhappiness.com/wp-content/themes/thehowofhappiness/Quiz/fit_diagnostic.html

I scored highest in 'Doing flow', and 'Cultivating optimism.' They match me perfectly, and taking the test helped me know myself better. This test has been proven to help us obtain greater happiness from the exercises above, as we can assign ourselves more confidently to the activities which suit us best.[339] This is the γνῶθι σεαυτόν (gnōthi seauton, literally 'know thyself') exercise that has been suggested since ancient Egyptian and Greek times.

Practice practice practice. We all know that it is no good to smoke, that most of us should sleep about eight hours or so, and that we should eat healthy and exercise. Happiness is common sense, but, perhaps more importantly, is converting into action the good you already know. This good has been the same for millennia, and particularly divulged in current culture by our major philosophers and religions.

Aristotle said that to be excellent we cannot simply think or feel excellent, we must act excellently. Virtue for him is the path of moderation between the extremes of excessive hedonism (materialism), versus asceticism. As my colleague Mike Foley said, to be happy is to live a life in harmony, so all cords are played to a nice tune.

Buddhism holds that happiness will be achieved by habitual practice of the virtues thought by masters, with exercise of the mind and will. Aristotle cultivates reason over emotions, while Buddha was more ascetic, but both held that practice of virtues was needed to achieve happiness. Even the Christian faith holds that virtue is achieved and strengthened by repetition of morally good acts, as said by Thomas Aquinas.

So form habits. Repeat the exercise at least once for twenty-one straight days.[340] Our brain actually changes in response to frequent, repeated, long-term practice. For example, crash dieters, who lose weight fast, regain weight much more than those who lose weight slowly, by changing their habits over a longer period of time.

There is no one secret to happiness, as there is no one perfect diet which makes everyone get to their ideal weight. For me, for example, it's most important to limit portions, and to have a small, not a large meal at night. I gain, or at least do not lose weight, by having too big or too many portions, and having lots of late big dinners.

Another scientifically proven way to form a habit is to make the action easier to do. For example, putting an exercise machine in front of the TV, instead of hidden away in a corner, makes the chance that one exercises much more probable. This is the same trick supermarkets play on us when they place the items they want us to buy at eye-level.[341]

Put the desired behavior on the path of least resistance, so it takes less effort and less energy. And raise the effort for habits you want to avoid. So hide the chocolate, and put fruits and vegetables everywhere in front of you. Healthy snacks should be all that's easily available in the house. Close your email. Put your sneakers out near the door.

Regarding happiness, I was born happy. But creating continuous challenges for myself, doing what I like, following the six intentional activities most associated with happiness, and systematically looking at the silver lining and bright side even in adversity, make me very happy.

Once you begin to get happier, the voluntary actions we have described, which have been scientifically proven to raise your level of happiness, will start a 'catch-22' process. Happier people are more naturally and spontaneously healthy, happily married, effective in their jobs, civic-minded, generous, and tolerant citizens,[342] who continue then to ever increase their satisfaction with life.

Some people unfortunately grow up to dislike themselves. They have no confidence. They have lost hope. Usually, this is for no good reason. It's just that they have not had when young a mentor to make them see the positive side of things, and to help them identify what they like to play best, what they should have practiced and concentrate on more, what therefore they could have mastered, and ultimately got recognition for. They did not have enough connectedness with a loved one. Consequently, they never realized whatever quality they had in them which would have made them, if cultivated, happy. They never discovered who they really are. And that is very sad.

A healthy relationship with yourself means that you feel content, most of the time, being who you are. You can interact with the world comfortable in your own skin, confident you may have something to contribute. This does not mean being selfish, or a narcissist. It just means that you may be anxious at times, but in general have no fear of interacting positively with others in almost all circumstances. Being yourself is no small achievement.

I sense that many people go through their whole life pretending to be somebody else. A tough husband. A dictator at work. A disciplinarian with kids. Refusing to dance. Avoiding crowds. Being afraid to speak in public. Perhaps that is not what they really are. But they never learned to shed whatever mechanism of defense they built when they were really young. Usually when they were less than 10 year old. Some decide to defend themselves by retreating. Some defend themselves by going on the harsh offence.

There are parts of me I'd like to improve. I forget things easily, especially those I pay no attention to. I love more by words that by acts, at times, and I could instead be less public and more factual in my giving out affection. I do like what I have done with my life to the point that I may appear 'too much' to others: too many awards, too many good things going for me, too much happiness. I could have maintained my curly black hair instead of going bald. I'd look much better with 10 pounds less on me. But I basically like who I am, and I accept myself, including the shortcomings. I still try to fight against flaws, but I'll never grow hair and I'll never surf again (probably).

I hope my children will continue to mature into adulthood comfortable about who they are. I hope they continue to strive to improve themselves, but also learn to play to their strengths, and accept who they are, and who they are going to become.

Appendix

The 24 strengths listed in 'Authentic happiness' (www.authentichappiness.com), by Martin Seligman, and how I did!

- WISDOM AND KNOWLEDGE
  - Curiosity
  - Love of learning
  - Judgment
  - Ingenuity
  - Social intelligence
  - Perspective
- COURAGE
  - Valor
  - Perseverance
  - Integrity
- HUMANITY AND LOVE
  - Kindness
  - Loving
- JUSTICE
  - Citizenship
  - Fairness
  - Leadership
- TEMPERANCE
  - Self-control
  - Prudence
  - Humility
- TRANSCENDENCE
  - Appreciation of beauty
  - Gratitude
  - Hope
  - Spirituality
  - Forgiveness
  - Humor
  - Zest

My top 10:

Top Strength
Industry, diligence, and perseverance
You work hard to finish what you start. No matter the project, you "get it out the door" in timely fashion. You do not get distracted when you work, and you take satisfaction in completing tasks.

Second Strength
Hope, optimism, and future-mindedness
You expect the best in the future, and you work to achieve it. You believe that the future is something that you can control.

Third Strength
Zest, enthusiasm, and energy
Regardless of what you do, you approach it with excitement and energy. You never do anything halfway or halfheartedly. For you, life is an adventure.

Fourth Strength
Curiosity and interest in the world
You are curious about everything. You are always asking questions, and you find all subjects and topics fascinating. You like exploration and discovery.

Fifth Strength
Perspective (wisdom)
Although you may not think of yourself as wise, your friends hold this view of you. They value your perspective on matters and turn to you for advice. You have a way of looking at the world that makes sense to others and to yourself.

Sixth Strength
Capacity to love and be loved
You value close relations with others, in particular those in which sharing and caring are reciprocated. The people to whom you feel most close are the same people who feel most close to you.

Seventh Strength
Fairness, equity, and justice
Treating all people fairly is one of your abiding principles. You do not let your personal feelings bias your decisions about other people. You give everyone a chance.

Eighth Strength
Humor and playfulness
You like to laugh and tease. Bringing smiles to other people is important to you. You try to see the light side of all situations.

Ninth Strength
Love of learning
You love learning new things, whether in a class or on your own. You have always loved school, reading, and museums-anywhere and everywhere there is an opportunity to learn.

Tenth Strength
Judgment, critical thinking, and open-mindedness
Thinking things through and examining them from all sides are important aspects of who you are. You do not jump to conclusions, and you rely only on solid evidence to make your decisions. You are able to change your mind.

REFERENCES

Introduction

[1] Aristotle. "Nichomachean Ethics", book 1, section 7.
[2] Diener, E. Subjective well-being: The science of happiness and a proposal for a national index. American Psychologist. 2000:55;34-43
[3] Diener, E., Suh, E.K., Smith H., and Shao, L. National differences in reported well-being: Why do they occur? Social Indicators Research. 1995;34:7-32.
[4] Helliwell J, Layard R, Sachs J. World Happiness Report 2013. New York: UN Sustainable Development Solutions Network.p.39.
[5] Kahneman D, Thaler RH. Anomalies, utility maximization, and experienced utility. Journal of economic perspectives. 2006;20:221
[6] Seligman MEP. (2002) Authentic happiness. New York. Free Press.
[7] Achor S. The happiness advantage. 2010. Crown business, Random House, New York.
[8] Lyubomirsky, S. The How of happiness. A New approach to getting the life you want. 2007. Penguin Books.
[9] Haidt L. The happiness hypothesis. 2006. Basic Books, New York.
[10] Hallowell EM. Childhood roots of adult happiness. 2002. Ballantine Books, Random House, New York.
[11] Bok D. The politics of happiness. 2010. Princeton University Press.
[12] Helliwell J, Layard R, Sachs J. World Happiness Report 2013. New York: UN Sustainable Development Solutions Network.
[13] Achor S. The happiness advantage. 2010. Crown business, Random House, New York.p.39.
[14] Bok D. The politics of happiness. 2010. Princeton University Press. p.48.
[15] Lyubomirsky, S. The How of happiness. A New approach to getting the life you want. 2007. Penguin Books.p.71.
[16] Mencius,6A:15 2A:2

Brief history of the pursuit of happiness

[17] Chan, Wing-tsit (1963). *A Source Book in Chinese Philosophy*. Princeton, NJ, US: Princeton University Press. ISBN 0691019649.
[18] Buddhist studies for primary and secondary students, Unit Six: The Four Immeasurables". Buddhanet.net. Retrieved 2013-04-26.
[19] SUMMA THEOLOGICA: Secunda Secundae Partis". Newadvent.org. Retrieved 2013-04-26.
[20] Levine, Marvin (2000). The Positive Psychology of Buddhism and Yoga : Paths to a Mature Happiness. Lawrence Erlbaum. ISBN 0805838333.
[21] McMahon DM. Happiness: a history. 2006;p. 200-21
[22] Bok D. The politics of happiness. 2010. Princeton University Press.
[23] Lyubomirsky, S. The How of happiness. A New approach to getting the life you want. 2007. Penguin Books.
[24] Achor S. The happiness advantage. 2010. Crown business, Random House, New York.p.39.
[25] Wordnet 3.0 (accessed 2011-Feb-24 via Wolfram Alpha)
[26] Fredrickson B. Positivity. 2009. Crown Publishers, New York.
[27] Lyubomirsky, S. The How of happiness. A New approach to getting the life you want. 2007. Penguin Books.p.32.

Happiness can be measured

[28] Helliwell J, Layard R, Sachs J. World Happiness Report 2013. New York: UN Sustainable Development Solutions Network.p.5.
http://www.oecd.org/statistics/Guidelines%20on%20Measuring%20Subjective%20Well-being.pdf)
[29] Helliwell J, Layard R, Sachs J. World Happiness Report 2013. New York: UN Sustainable Development Solutions Network.
[30] Gallup World Poll (GWP), see http://www.gallup.com/poll/122453/understanding-gallup-uses-cantril-scale.aspx (reviewed 10/31/2013)
[31] Used in the World Values Survey, the Europena Social Survey, and many other national and international surveys.

[32] Helliwell J, Layard R, Sachs J. World Happiness Report 2013. New York: UN Sustainable Development Solutions Network.p.3.
[33] Lyubomirsky S, Lepper HS. A measure of subjective happiness: preliminary reliability and construct validation. Social indicators research 1999;46:137-55. http://sonjalyubomirsky.com/subjective-happiness-scale-shs/
[34] Dunn E, Aknin LB, Norton MI. Spending money on others promotes happiness. Science 2008;319:1687-8.
[35] Bok D. The politics of happiness. 2010. Princeton University Press. p.32-38.
[36] Sandvick E, Diener E, Seidlitz L. Subjective well-being: the convergence and stability of self-report and non-self report measures. Journal of Personality 1993;61:317.
[37] Keltner D, Harker LA. Expression of positive emotion in women's college yearbook pictures and their relationship to personality and life outcomes across adulthood. Journal of Personality and Social Psychology 2001;80:112.
[38] Lyubomirsky S, Knight L, Diener E. The benefits of frequent positive affect: does happiness lead to success? Psychological Bulletin 2005;131:803.
[39] Helliwell J, Layard R, Sachs J. World Happiness Report 2013. New York: UN Sustainable Development Solutions Network.p.139.
[40] Helliwell J, Layard R, Sachs J. World Happiness Report 2013. New York: UN Sustainable Development Solutions Network.p.139-151.
[41] Helliwell J, Layard R, Sachs J. World Happiness Report 2013. New York: UN Sustainable Development Solutions Network.p.4.

<u>What determines happiness?</u>
[42] Lyubomirsky S, Sheldon KM, Schkade D. Pursuing happiness: the architecture of sustainable change. Review of General Psychology. 2005;9:111-31.
[43] Lyubomirsky, S. The How of happiness. A New approach to getting the life you want. 2007. Penguin Books.
[44] Lykken D, tellegen A. Happiness is a stochastic phenomenon. Psychological Science 1996;7:186-9.
[45] Caspi Sugden K, Moffitt TE, Taylor A, Craig IW, Harrington HL, et al. Influence of life stress on depression: moderation by a polymorphism in the 5-HTT gene. Science 2003;301:386-9.
[46] Taylor SE, Way BM, Welch WT, et al. Early family development, current adversity, the serotonin transporter promoter polymorphism, and depressive symptomatology. Biological Psychiatry 2006;60:671-6.
[47] Tomarken AJ, Davidson RJ, Wheeler RE, Doss RC. Individual differences in anterior brain asymmetry and fundamenta dimensions of emotion. Journal of Personality and Social Psychology 1992;62:676-87.
[48] Urry HL, Nitschke JB, Dolski I, et al. Making a life worth living: neural correlates of well-being. Psychological Science 2004;15:367-72.
[49] Stallone DD, Stunkard AJ. The regulation of body weight: evidence and clinical implications. Annals of behavioral medicine. 1991;13:220-30.
[50] Lyubomirsky, S. The How of happiness. A New approach to getting the life you want. 2007. Penguin Books.p.40.
[51] Diener E, Suh EM, Lucas RE, Smith HL. Subjective well-being: three decades of progress. Psychological Bulletin. 1999;125: 276-302.
[52] Lyubomirsky, S. The How of happiness. A New approach to getting the life you want. 2007. Penguin Books.p.41.
[53] Maslow A. Motivation and personalty. 170. 2nd edition. Harper and Row.
[54] Lyubomirsky, S. The How of happiness. A New approach to getting the life you want. 2007. Penguin Books.p.318.
[55] Biswas-Diener R, Diener E. Making the best of a bad situation: satisfaction in the slums of Calcutta. Social Indicators Research 2001;55:329-52.
[56] Shakespeare W. Hamlet, II.ii.249-0. In G Blakemore (Ed), The Riverside Shakespeare, 1974. Houghton Mifflin, Boston.

<u>Your attitude</u>
[57] Foley MR. Ancient wisdom for life fulfillment. 2010. Chaos Publishing Co., Paradise Valley, AZ.

[58] Ricard, M. (2007). Happiness: A guide to developing life's most important skill. New York: Little, Brown and Company.p.19.
[59] Diener E, Sandvik E, Pavor W. Happiness is the frequency, not the intensity, of positive versus negative affect. In Strack F, Argyle M, Scwartz N. Subjective well-being: An interdispiplinary prospective. 1991. Elmsford, NY: Pergamon.

<u>The six intentional activities which create happiness</u>
[60] Seligman MEP. (2002) Authentic happiness. New York. Free Press.
[61] Denier E, Biswas-Diener R. Happiness: unlocking the mysteries of psychological wealth. 2008;p.47-67.
[62] Valliant G. Yes, I stand by my words, "Happiness equals love – full stop." Positive Psychology News daily, in http://positivepsychologynews.com/news/george-valient/200907163163.
[63] Diener E, Seligman M. Very happy people. Psychological Science 2002;13:81-4.
[64] Haidt L. The happiness hypothesis. 2006. Basic Books, New York.
[65] Helliwell JF, Putnam RD. The social context of well-being, in: Huppert FA, Baylis N, Keverne B. The science of well-being. 2007;p.435.
[66] Spiegel D, et al. Effect of psychosocial treatment on survival of patients with metastatic breast cancer. The Lancet 1989;2:888-91.
[67] Wing RR, Jeffery RW. Benefits of recruiting participants with friends and increasing social support for weight loss and maintenance. Journal of consulting and clinical psychology 1999;67:132-8.
[68] Thompson C. Are you friends making you fat? New York Times, September 10, 2009.
[69] Totterdell P. Catching moods and hitting runs: mood linkage and subjective performance in professional sport teams. Journal of Applied Psychology 2000;85:848-59.
[70] Holahan CK, Sear RR. The gifted group in later maturity. Stanford University Press, Palo Alto, CA.
[71] Campion MA, Papper EM, Medsker GJ. Relations between work team characteristics and effectiveness: a replication and extension. Personnel Psychology 1996;49:429-52.
[72] Heaphy E, Dutton JE. Positive social interactions and the human body at work: linking organizations and physiology. Academy of Management review 2008;33:137-62.
[73] Buckingham M, Coffman C. First, break all the rules. 1999. Simon and Schuster, New York.
[74] Wagner N, Feldman G, Hussy T. The effect of ambulatory blood pressure on working under favorably and unfavorably perceived supervisors. Occupational Environmental Medicine 2003;60:468-74.
[75] Foley MR. Ancient wisdom for life fulfillment. 2010. Chaos Publishing Co., Paradise Valley, AZ.
[76] Foley MR. Ancient wisdom for life fulfillment. 2010. Chaos Publishing Co., Paradise Valley, AZ.
[77] Achor S. The happiness advantage. 2010. Crown business, Random House, New York.p.177.
[78] Cacioppo JT. Loneliness: human nature and the need for social connections. WW Norton and Co., New York
[79] Disraeli B. Lothair. Cambridge, UK, 2000.p.206.
[80] Cantor N, Sanderson CA. Life task participation and well-being: The importance of taking part in daily life. In Kahnemann et al. 1999, p.230-43.
[81] Wolfe WB. How to be happy through human. 2001. London: Routledge.
[82] Lyubomirsky, S. The How of happiness. A New approach to getting the life you want. 2007. Penguin Books.p.205.
[83] Brunstein JC. Personal goals and subjective well-being: a longitudinal study. Journal of Personal and Social Psychology 1993;65:1061-70.
[84] Aristotle, Nichomachean Ethics, bk. 1, 1094a.
[85] Sheldon KM. When personal goals correctly represent the person. In: Deci EL, Ryan RM. Handbook of self-determination theory. 2002. Rochester, NY: University of Rochester Press.
[86] Lyubomirsky, S. The How of happiness. A New approach to getting the life you want. 2007. Penguin Books.p.210.
[87] Elliot AJ, Sheldon KM. Avoidance personal goals and the personality-illness relationship. Journal of Personality and Social Psychology 1998;75:1282-99.
[88] Norcross JC, Mrykalo MS, Blagys MD. Auld Lang Syne: Success predictors, change processes, and self-reported outcomes of New Year's resolvers and nonresolvers. Journal of Clinical Psychology 2002;58:397-405.
[89] Lepper MR, Greene D, Nisbett RE. Undermining children's intrinsic interest with extrinsic reward: a test of the 'overjustification' hypothesis. Journal of personality and Social Psychology 1973;28:129-37.

[90] Wrzesniewski A., McCauley C, Rozin P, Scwartz B. Jobs, careers, and callings: people's relations to their work. Journal of Research in Personality;1997:31:21-3.
[91] Seligman MEP. (2002) Authentic happiness. New York. Free Press. p.168
[92] Reader's Digest, June 2013, p.105.
[93] Wrzesniewski A., Rozin, Bennett. 2003.
[94] Achor S. The happiness advantage. 2010. Crown business, Random House, New York.p.80.
[95] Haidt J. The happiness hypothesis. 2006. Basic Books, New York.
[96] Seligman MEP. (2002) Authentic happiness. New York. Free Press. p.177
[97] Eaton WW, Anthony J, Mandel W, Garrision R. Occupations and the prevalence of major depressive disorder. Journal of Occupational Medicine 1990;32:1079-87.
[98] Haidt J. The happiness hypothesis. 2006. Basic Books, New York.p.219.
[99] Leo Tolstoy, quoted in Troyat, 1967, 158.
[100] Seligman MEP. (2002) Authentic happiness. New York. Free Press.
[101] Gladwell M. Outliers. 2008. Little, Brown and Company, New York.
[102] Seligman MEP. (2002) Authentic happiness. New York. Free Press. p.93
[103] Seligman MEP. Learned optimism. 1991. Knopf, New York.p.152-3.
[104] Shakespeare. Troilus and Cressida, I.ii.287.
[105] Seligman MEP. (2002) Authentic happiness. New York. Free Press.

Other intentional activities associated with happiness
[106] Bok D. The politics of happiness. 2010. Princeton University Press.
[107] Seligman MEP. (2002) Authentic happiness. New York. Free Press.
[108] Harker and Keltner, 2001.
[109] Stutzer A, Frey BS. Does marriage make people happy or do happy people get married? Journal of Socio-Economics 2006;35:326.
[110] Myers DG. Close relationships and the quality of life, in Kahleman D, Diener E, Schwartz N. Well-being: the foundation of hedonic psychology 1999;p.374, 380.
[111] Inglehart R. Culture shift in advanced industrial society. 1990. Princeton, NJ: Princeton University Press.
[112] De Paulo BM, Morris WL. Singles in society and in science. Psychological inquiry.2005;16:57-83.
[113] Myer D. The American paradox. 2000. New Haven, CT: Yale University Press.
[114] Myer D. The American paradox. 2000. New Haven, CT: Yale University Press.
[115] Frey BS. Happiness: a revolution in economics. 2008.
[116] Lucas RE, Clark AE. Do people really adapt to marriage? Journal of Happiness Studies 2006;7:405.
[117] Lyubomirsky, S. The How of happiness. A New approach to getting the life you want. 2007. Penguin Books.p.65.
[118] Lucas RE. Time does not heal all wounds: a longitudinal study of reaction and adaptation to divorce. Psychological science 2005;16:945.
[119] Lucas RE. Time does not heal all wounds: a longitudinal study of reaction and adaptation to divorce. Psychological science 2005;16:945.
[120] Horn WF. Marriage, family, and the welfare of children: a call for action, in: Maynihan DP. Smeeding TM, Rainwater L. The future of the family, 2004,p.185.
[121] Myer D. The American paradox. 2000. New Haven, CT: Yale University Press.
[122] Tait M, Padgett MY, Baldwin TT. Job and life satisfaction: a reevaluation of the strength of the relationship and gender effects as a function of the date of the study. Journal of Applied Psychology 1989;74:502.
[123] Rain JS, Lane IM, Steiner DD. A current look at the job satisfaction / life satisfaction relationship: re view and future considerations. Human Relations 1991;44:287.
[124] Helliwell JF, Huang H. How's the job? Well-being and social capital in the workplace. National Bureau of Economic Research, Working Paper No. 11759. 2005.
[125] Helliwell JF, Huang H, Putman RP. Are trust and social capital neglected workplace investments? (unpublished paper, 2008, reported in: Bok D. The politics of happiness. 2010. Princeton University Press. p.218.
[126] Judge TA, Watanabe S. Another look at the job satisfaction-lifge stasfaction relationship. Journal of Applied Psychology 1993;78:939.

[127] Wrzesniewski A., McCauley C, Rozin P, Scwartz B. Jobs, careers, and callings: people's relations to their work. Journal of Research in Personality;1997:31:21-3.
[128] Bok D. The politics of happiness. 2010. Princeton University Press. p.29.
[129] Lyubomirsky, S. The How of happiness. A New approach to getting the life you want. 2007. Penguin Books. P.188
[130] DeWitte H. Job insecurity and well-being: review of the literature and explanation of some unresolved issues. European Journal of Work and Organizational Psychology 1999;8:155.
[131] Bok D. The politics of happiness. 2010. Princeton University Press. p.114.
[132] Nettles D. Happiness: the science behind your smile. 2005;p.111.
[133] Lucas RE, Clark AE, Georgellis Y, Diener E. Unemployment alters the set point of life satisfaction. Psychological Science 2004;15:18.
[134] National Opinion Research Center survey, quoted by Elisabeth Warren, Unsafe at any rate. Democracy Journal, summer 2007, p.11.
[135] Layard R. Happiness: lessons from a new science. 2005. P.64.
[136] Bok D. The politics of happiness. 2010. Princeton University Press. p.21.
[137] Brickman P, Coates D, Janoff-Buhlman R. Lottery winners and accident victims: is happiness relative? Journal of Personality and Social Psychology 1978;2:917.
[138] Lyubomirsky, S. The How of happiness. A New approach to getting the life you want. 2007. Penguin Books.p.51.
[139] Riis J, Loewenstein G, Baron J, Jepson C, fagerlin A, Ubel PA. Ignorance of edonic adaptation to hemodyalisis: a study using ecological momentary assessment. Journal of Experimental Psychology: General 2005;134:3-9.
[140] Ratey JJ, Hagerman E. Spark: the revolutionary new science of exercise and the brain, 2008.
[141] Kahneman D, Riis J. Living and thinking about it: two perspectives on life, in Huppert FA, Baylis N, Keverne B. The science of well-being. 2007;p285,295.
[142] Frey BS, Stutzer A. Happiness research: state and prospects. Review of Social Economy 2005;62:207, 213.
[143] Dunn EW, Aknin LB, Norton MI. Spending money on others. Science 2008;319:1687.
[144] Thoits PA, Hewitt LN. Volunteer work and well-being. Journal of Health ans Social behavior 2001;42:115.
[145] Carnegie A. Gospel of Wealth.
[146] Haidt J. The happiness hypothesis. Basic Books, New York.
[147] Harlow and Zimmerman, 1959.
[148] Bible. Paul, Letter to the Romans, 5:3-4.
[149] Haidt J. The happiness hypothesis. Basic Books, New York.
[150] Pennbaker J. Opening up.1997.
[151] Layard R. Happiness: lessons from a new science. 2005. P.64.
[152] Myers DG. The pursuit of happiness: discovering the pathway to fulfillment, well-being, and enduring personal joy. 1992;p.183.
[153] Ferris AL. Religion and the quality of life. Journal of Happiness Studies 2002;3:199.
[154] Inglehart R. Democracy and happiness: what causes what? Paper presented at Notre Dame conference on New directions in the study of happiness, October 2006.
[155] Inglehart R, Foa R, Peterson C, Welzel C. Development, freedom, and rising happiness: a global perspective (1981-2007). Perspectives on Psychological Science 2008;3:264.
[156] Inglehart R, Foa R, Peterson C, Welzel C. Development, freedom, and rising happiness: a global perspective (1981-2007). Perspectives on Psychological Science 2008;3:271.
[157] Helliwell J, Layard R, Sachs J. World Happiness Report 2013. New York: UN Sustainable Development Solutions Network.p.22.
[158] Helliwell J, Layard R, Sachs J. World Happiness Report 2013. New York: UN Sustainable Development Solutions Network.p.9.
[159] Helliwell J, Layard R, Sachs J. World Happiness Report 2013. New York: UN Sustainable Development Solutions Network.p.81.
[160] Helliwell J, Layard R, Sachs J. World Happiness Report 2013. New York: UN Sustainable Development Solutions Network.p.82.
[161] Bok D. The politics of happiness. 2010. Princeton University Press. p.78.

[162] Helliwell J, Layard R, Sachs J. World Happiness Report 2013. New York: UN Sustainable Development Solutions Network.p.16.
[163] Alesina A, Angeletos GM. Fairness and redistribution. American Economic Review 2005;95:960,965.
[164] Bok D. The politics of happiness. 2010. Princeton University Press.
[165] Helliwell J, Layard R, Sachs J. World Happiness Report 2013. New York: UN Sustainable Development Solutions Network.p.24.
[166] Helliwell J, Layard R, Sachs J. World Happiness Report 2013. New York: UN Sustainable Development Solutions Network.p.102.

Factors with modest impact on happiness
[167] DiTella R, MacCulloch RJ, Oswald AJ. The macroeconomics of happiness. Review of economics and statistics. 2003;85:809.
[168] Alesina A, Glaeser EL. Fighting poverty in the US and Europe: a world of difference. 2004,p.184.
[169] Alesina A, Glaeser EL. Fighting poverty in the US and Europe: a world of difference. 2004,p.184.
[170] Bok D. The politics of happiness. 2010. Princeton University Press, p.81.
[171] Easterling RA. Does economic growth improve the human lot? Some empirical evidence, in David PA, Reder MW. Nations and households in economic growth: essays in honor of Moses Abramowitz. 1974;p. 89.
[172] Easterling RA. Feeding the illusion of happiness: a reply to Hagerty and Veehoven. Social indicators research. 2005;p. 74.
[173] Diener E, Suh EM, Kucas RE, Smith HL. Subjective well-being: three decades of progress. 1999;125:276 and 292.
[174] Easterling RA. Feeding the illusion of happiness: a reply to Hagerty and Veehoven. Social indicators research. 2005; p. 74.
[175] Di Tella R, MacCulloch R. Happiness adaptation to income beyond basic needs. Draft paper for Princeton Conference on International Differences in Well-Being. 2008;p.7.
[176] Schor JB. The overspent American: why we want what we do not need. 1998;p.15.
[177] Luttmer EFP. Neighbors as negatives: relative earnings and well-being. Quarterly Journal of Economics 2005;121:963.
[178] Haidt J. The Happiness hypothesis. 2006. Basic Books, New York.
[179] Time magazine, July 8-15, 2013, p. 30, based on studies in the Journal of Positive Psychology.
[180] Denier E, Biswas-Diener R. Happiness: unlocking the mysteries of psychological wealth. 2008;p73.
[181] Bok D. The politics of happiness. 2010. Princeton University Press.
[182] Bok D. The politics of happiness. 2010. Princeton University Press.
[183] Kasser T, Kanner AD. Psychology of consumer culture: the struggle for a good life in a materialistic world. 2004.
[184] Nickerson C, Schwartz N, Diener E, Kahneman. Zeroing in on the dark side of the American dream. Psychological science 2003;14:535.
[185] Nickerson C, Schwartz N, Diener E, Kahneman. Zeroing in on the dark side of the American dream. Psychological science 2003;14:531-6.
[186] Kahneman D, Krueger AB, Schkade D, Schwatrz N, Stone AA. Would you be happier if you were richer? A focusing illusion. Science 2006;312:1908-10.
[187] Cohen P, Cohen J. Life values and adolescent mental health. Mahwah, NJ: Erlbaum, 1996.
[188] Harwood Group. Yearning for balance: views of Americans on consumption, materialism, and the environment. 1995, www.iisd.ca/consume.harwood.html.
[189] Oishi S, Diener E, Lucas E. The optimal level of well-being: can people be too happy? Perspectives on Psychological Science 2007;2:346.
[190] Kasser T, Kanner AD. Psychology of consumer culture: the struggle for a good life in a materialistic world. 2004.
[191] Ross CE, Van Willigen M. Education and the subjective quality of life. Journal of Health and Social Behavior 1997;38:275.
[192] Nomaguchi K, Milkie MA. Costs and rewards of children: the effects of becoming a parent on adults' lives. Journal of Marriage and the Family 2003;65:356.
[193] Somers MD. A comparison of voluntarily child-free adults and parents. Journal of Marriage and the Family 1993;55:643.

[194] Bok D. The politics of happiness. 2010. Princeton University Press, p.19.
[195] Lehman DR, Wortman CB, Williams AF. Long term effects of losing a spouse or child in a motor vehicle crash. Journal of Personality and Social Psychology 1987;52:218.

Factors not associated with happiness
[196] Argyle M. The psychology of happiness. 2001;p.105, 125.
[197] Frederick S, Loewenstein G. Hedonic adaptation. In Kahneman D, Diener E, Schwartz N (eds). Well-being: the foundations of hedonic psychology. New York: Russell Sage. 1999;p.353-75.
[198] Donovan N, Halpern D. Life satisfaction: the state of knowledge and implications of government 2002;p.5,25.
[199] Robinson JP, Godbey G. Time for life: the surprising ways Americans use their time. 1997;p.242.
[200] Lyubomirsky, S. The How of happiness. A New approach to getting the life you want. 2007. Penguin Books. P.187
[201] Bok D. The politics of happiness. 2010. Princeton University Press, p.206.
[202] Foley MR. Ancient wisdom for life fulfillment. 2010. Chaos Publishing Co., Paradise Valley, AZ.
[203] Time magazine, July 8-15, 2013, p. 31, based on studies in several sources.
[204] Diener E, Wolsic B, Fujita E. Physical attractiveness and subjective well-being. Journal of Personality and Social Psychology 1995;69:120-29.
[205] Meyer B, Enstrom MK, Harstveit M, Bowles DP, Beevers CG. Happiness and despair on the catwalk: need satisfaction, well-being, and personality adjustment among fashion models. Journal of Positive Psychology 2007;2:2-17.
[206] Argyle M. Causes and correlates of happiness. In Kahneman D, Diener E, Schwartz N (eds). Well-being: the foundations of hedonic psychology. New York: Russell Sage. 1999;p.353-75.
[207] Stevenson B, Wolfers J. The paradox of declining female happiness. American Economic Journal: Economic Policy. 2011.
[208] Diener E, Suh ME. Subjective well-being and age: an international analysis. Annual Review of Gerontology and Geriatrics 1997;p.304.
[209] Yang Y. Social inequalities in happiness in the United States, 1972-2004: an age-period cohort analysis 2008;73:204-20.
[210] Mroczek DK, Spiro A. Change in life satisfaction during adulthood: findings from the Veteran Affairs Normative Aging Study. Journal of Personality and Socila Psychology 2005;88:189-202.
[211] Langer E. Counterclockwise: mindful health and the power of possibility. 2009. Ballantine: New York.
[212] Haslam SA, Salvatore J, Kessler T, reicher SD. How stereotyping yourself contributes to your success (or failure). Scientific American Mind, March 4, 2008.
[213] Brickman P, Coates D, Janoff-Bulman R. Lottery winners and accident victims: is happiness relative? Journal of Personality and Social Psychology 1978;36:917-27.

Factors associated with unhappiness
[214] Frank, 1999.
[215] Koslowsky and Kluger, 1995.
[216] Bok D. The politics of happiness. 2010. Princeton University Press. p.29.
[217] Frederick and Loewenstein, 1999.
[218] Yang Y. Social inequalities in happiness in the United States, 1972-2004: an age-period cohort analysis 2008;73:218-20.

Childhood roots of adult happiness
[219] Hallowell EM. Childhood roots of adult happiness. 2002. Ballantine Books, Random House, New York.
[220] Haidt J. The happiness hypothesis. 2006. Basic Books, New York.
[221] Fitzgerald, 1988.
[222] Mihaly Csikszentmihalyi. Finding Flow: The Psychology of Engagement with Everyday Life. 1998. Mastermind Series.
[223] Ken Robinson and Lou Aronica. Finding Your Element: How to Discover Your Talents and Passions and Transform Your Life. 2003.
[224] Gardner, Csikszentmihalyi, Damon. 2001.

[225] Brickman P, Coates D, Janoff-Bulman R. Lottery winners and accident victims: is happiness relative? Journal of Personality and Social Psychology 1978;36:917-27.
[226] Linley PA, Joseph S. Positive change following trauma and adversity: a review. Journal of Traumatic Stress 2004;17:11-21.
[227] Deci EL. Why we do what we do. 1996. Penguin, New York.
[228] Losada M, Heaphy E. The role of positivity and connectivity in the performance of business teams: a nonlinear dynamics model. American Behavioral Scientist 2004;47:740-65.
[229] Haidt J. The happiness hypothesis. 2006. Basic Books, New York.

Parent for happiness
[230] Hallowell EM. Childhood roots of adult happiness. 2002. Ballantine Books, Random House, New York.
[231] Russek LG, Schwartz GE. Perceptions of parental caring predict health status in mid-life: a 35-year follow-up of the Harvard Masery of Stress study. Psychosomatic Medicine 1997;59:144.
[232] Seligman MEP. (2002) Authentic happiness. New York. Free Press. p.11.
[233] Global Ethic Foundation. (2009). Global economic ethic — Consequences for global businesses. Retrieved from http://www.globaleconomicethic.org/
[234] Kaplan KA. College faces mental health crisis. The Harvard Crisom, January 12, 2004.
[235] Hallowell EM. Childhood roots of adult happiness. 2002. Ballantine Books, Random House, New York.
[236] Achor S. The happiness advantage. 2010. Crown business, Random House, New York.p.13.
[237] Achor S. The happiness advantage. 2010. Crown business, Random House, New York.p.13.
[238] Rosenthal R, Jacobson L. Pygmalion in the classroom: teacher expectation and pupils' intellectual development. 1968. Holt, Rinehart and Wiston, New York.

Benefits of happiness
[239] Lyubomirsky, S., King, L., and Diener, E. The benefits of frequent positive affect: Does happiness lead to success? Psychological Bulletin. 2005;131:803-55.
[240] Helliwell J, Layard R, Sachs J. World Happiness Report 2013. New York: UN Sustainable Development Solutions Network.p.56-7.
[241] Lyubomirsky, S., King, L., and Diener, E. The benefits of frequent positive affect: Does happiness lead to success? Psychological Bulletin. 2005;131:803-55.
[242] Seligman MEP. (2002) Authentic happiness. New York. Free Press. p.43
[243] Achor S. The happiness advantage. 2010. Crown business, Random House, New York.
[244] Achor S. The happiness advantage. 2010. Crown business, Random House, New York.p.15.
[245] Achor S. The happiness advantage. 2010. Crown business, Random House, New York.p.44.
[246] Bryan T, Bryan J. Positive mood and math performance. Journal of Learning Disabilities 1991;24:490-4.
[247] Kopelman S, Rosette AS, Thompson L. The three faces of Eve: strategic displays of positive, negative, and neutral emotions in negotiations. Organizational Behavior and Human Decision Processes 2006;99:81-101.
[248] Greenberg MH, Arakawa D. Optimistic managers and their influence on productivity and employee engagement in a technology organization. As cited by: Robinson J. The business benefits of a positive leader. Gallup Management Journal, May 10, 2007.
[249] Felps, W., Mitchell, T. R., & Byington, E. (2006). How, when, and why bad apples spoil the barrel: Negative group members and dysfunctional groups. Research in Organizational Behavior: An Annual Review Series of Analytic Essays and Critical Reviews, 27, 175-222.
[250] Diener, E., & Seligman, M. E. P. (2002). Very happy people. *Psychological Science, 13,* 81-84.
[251] Harker L, Keltner D. Expression of positive emotions in women's college yearbook pictures and their relationship to personality and life outcomes across adulthood. Journal of Personality and Social Psychology. 2001; 80:112-24.
[252] Johnson, K. J., & Fredrickson, B. L. (2005). "We all look the same to me:" Positive emotions eliminate the own-race bias in face recognition. Psychological Science, 16, 875-881.
[253] Carnevale, P. J. (2008). Positive effect and decision frame in negotiation. Group Decision and Negotiation, 17, 51-63.
[254] Guven, C. (2012). Reversing the question: Does happiness affect consumption and savings behavior? Journal of Economic Psychology, 33(4), 701-717.

[255] Aknin, L. B., Barrington-Leigh, C. P., Dunn, E. W., Helliwell, J. F., Biswas-Diener, R., Kemeza, I., Nyende, P., Ashton-James, C. E., & Norton, M. I. (2013). Prosocial spending and wellbeing: Cross-cultural evidence for a psychological universal. Journal of Personality and Social Psychology, 104, 635-652.
[256] Oishi, S., Diener, E., & Lucas, R. (2007). The optimum level of well-being: Can people be too happy? Perspectives on Psychological Science, 2, 346–360.
[257] Ifcher, J., & Zarghamee, H. (2011a). Happiness and time preference: The effect of positive affect in a random assignment experiment. American Economic Review, 101(7), 3109-3129.
[258] Aspinwall, L. G. (1998). Rethinking the role of positive affect in self-regulation. Motivation and Emotion, 22, 1-32.
[259] Gallup-Healthways Well-Being Index. June 18, 2008, in Associated Press.
[260] Peterson, S. J., Luthans, F., Avolio, B. J., Walumbwa, F. O., & Zhang, Z. (2011). Psychological capital and employee performance: A latent growth modeling approach. Personnel Psychology, 64, 427-450.
[261] Achor S. The happiness advantage. 2010. Crown business, Random House, New York.p.37.
[262] Lyobomirsky S, King L, Diener E. The benefits of frequent positive affect: does happiness lead to success? Psychological Bulletin 2005;131:803-855.
[263] Krause, Annabelle (2012). Don't worry, be happy? Happiness and reemployment. Discussion Paper Series, Forschungsinstitut zur Zukunft der Arbeit, No. 7107.
[264] Denier E, Nickelson C, Lucas RE, Sandvik E. Dispositional affect and job outcomes. Social Indicators Research. 2002;59:229-59.
[265] Staw B, Sutton R, Pelled L. Employee positive emotion and favorable outcomes at the workplace. Organizational Science 1994;5:51-71.
[266] Diener, E., Nickerson, C., Lucas, R. E., & Sandvik, E. (2002). Dispositional affect and job outcomes. Social Indicators… Research, 59, 229-259.
[267] De Neve, J.-E., & Oswald, A. J. (2012). Estimating the influence of life satisfaction and positive affect on later income using sibling fixed effects. PNAS: Proceedings of the National Academy of Sciences, 109(49), 19953-19958.
[268] Gallagher W. Rapt. 2009. Penguin, New York. p.36.
[269] Ong, A. D. Pathways linking positive emotion and health in later life. Current Directions in Psychological Science 2010;19:358-362.
[270] Davidson, K. W., Mostofsky, E., & Whang, W. (2010). Don't worry, be happy: Positive affect and reduced 10-year incident coronary heart disease: The Canadian Nova Scotia health survey. European Heart Journal, 31, 1065-1070.
[271] Boehm, J. K., & Kubzansky, L. D. (2012). The heart's content: The association between positive psychological well-being and cardiovascular health. Psychological Bulletin, 138, 655-691.
[272] Cohen S, Doyle WJ, Turner RB, Alper CM, Skoner DP. Emotional style and susceptibility to the common cold. Psycosomatic Medicine 2003;65:652-7.
[273] Appleton, A. A. Buka, S. L., McCormick, M. C., Koenen, K. C., Loucks, E. B., Gilman, S. E., & Kubzansky, L. D. Emotional functioning at age 7 years is associated with C-reactive protein in middle adulthood. Psychosomatic Medicine 2011; 73: 295-303.
[274] Fredrickson BL. The role of positive emotions in positive psychology: the broaden-and-built theory of positive emotions. American Psychologist 2001;56:218-26.
[275] Pettay, R. S. (2008). Health behaviors and life satisfaction in college students. Doctoral Dissertation, Kansas State University.
[276] Goudie, R., Mukherjee, S., De Neve, J.-E., Oswald, A. J., & Wu, S. (forthcoming). Happiness as a driver of risk-avoiding behavior: A conceptual framework with an application to seatbelt wearing and automobile accidents. Economica.
[277] Bray, I., & Gunnell, D. (2006). Suicide rates, life satisfaction and happiness as markers for population mental health. Social Psychiatry and Psychiatric Epidemiology, 41, 333-337.
[278] Rasmussen, H. N., Scheier, M. F., & Greenhouse, J. B. (2009). Optimism and physical health: A review. Annals of Behavioral Medicine, 37, 239-256.
[279] Fredrickson, B. L., & Levenson, R. W. (1998). Positive emotions speed recovery from the cardiovascular sequelae of negative emotions. Cognition and Emotion, 12, 191-220.
[280] Danner, D. D., Snowdon, D. A., & Friesen, W. V. (2001). Positive emotions in early life and longevity: Findings from the nun study. Journal of Personality and Social Psychology, 80, 804-813.

[281] Seligman MEP. (2002) Authentic happiness. New York. Free Press. p.4.
[282] Chida, Y., & Steptoe, A. (2008). Positive psychological wellbeing and mortality: A quantitative review of prospective observational studies. Psychosomatic Medicine, 70, 741-756.
[283] Epel, E. S., Blackburn, E. H., Liu, J., Dhabhar, F. S., Adler, N. E., Morrow, J. D., & Cawthon, R. M. (2004). Accelerated telomere shortening in response to life stress. PNAS: Proceedings of the National Academy of Sciences, 101(49), 17323–17324.
[284] Achor S. The happiness advantage. 2010. Crown business, Random House, New York.p.17.
[285] Achor S. The happiness advantage. 2010. Crown business, Random House, New York.p.17.

Your happiness depends on you
[286] Buddha. Dhammapada, verse 1, in Mascaro, 1973.
[287] Achor S. The happiness advantage. 2010. Crown business, Random House, New York.p.71.
[288] Crum AJ, Langer EJ. Mindset matters: exercise and the placebo effect. Psychological Science 2007;18:165-71.
[289] Fredrickson, B. L., Grewen, K. M., Coffey, K. A., Algoe, S. B., Firestine, A. M., Arevalo, J. M. G., . . . Cole, S. W. (2013). A functional genomic perspective on human well-being. PNAS: Proceedings of the National Academy of Sciences, doi:10.1073/pnas.1305419110.
[290] Hallowell EM. Childhood roots of adult happiness. 2002. Ballantine Books, Random House, New York.p.69.
[291] Sparr JL, Sonnetag S. Feedback environment and well-being at work: the mediating role of personal control and feelings of helplessness. European Journal of Work and Organizational Psychology 2008;17:388-412.
[292] Rodin J, Langer EJ. Long-term effects of a control-relevant intervention with the institutionalized aged. Journal of Personality and Social Psychology 1977;35:897-902.
[293] Lyubomirsky, S. The How of happiness. A New approach to getting the life you want. 2007. Penguin Books.
[294] Boethius, 1962/c. 522 CE, 29.
[295] Achor S. The happiness advantage. 2010. Crown business, Random House, New York.p.63.
[296] Achor S. The happiness advantage. 2010. Crown business, Random House, New York.p.64-5.
[297] Lyubomirsky, S. The How of happiness. A New approach to getting the life you want. 2007. Penguin Books.p.64.

Happiness practice exercises
[298] Hansen, 1991.
[299] Aristotle, 1962/4th cent. BCE, 1003b.
[300] Lyubomirsky, S. The How of happiness. A New approach to getting the life you want. 2007. Penguin Books.
[301] Zajonk RB, Murphy ST, Inglehart M. Feeling and facial efference: implications for the vascular theory of emotion. Psychological Review 1898;96:395-416.
[302] Christakis NA, Fowler J. Connected. 2009. Little, Brown, and Co., New York.
[303] Iacoboni M. Mirroring people. 2008. Picador, New York.
[304] Seligman MEP. (2002) Authentic happiness. New York. Free Press. p.35
[305] Friedman H, Riggio R. Effect of individual differences in nonverbal expressiveness on transmission of emotion. Journal of Nonverbal Behavior 1981;6:96-104.
[306] Achor S. The happiness advantage. 2010. Crown business, Random House, New York.p.118.
[307] Lyubomirsky, S. The How of happiness. A New approach to getting the life you want. 2007. Penguin Books.
[308] Achor S. The happiness advantage. 2010. Crown business, Random House, New York.p.206.
[309] Seligman MEP. (2002) Authentic happiness. New York. Free Press
[310] Seligman MEP. (2002) Authentic happiness. New York. Free Press
[311] Bryant F, Veroff J. Savoring: A new model of Positive Experience. 2006. Mahwah, NJ: Erlbaum.
[312] Bryant F, Veroff J. Savoring: A new model of Positive Experience. 2006. Mahwah, NJ: Erlbaum.
[313] Post SG. Altruism, happiness, and health: it's good to be good. International Journal of Behavioral Medicine 2005;12:66-77.

[314] Scwartz et al. Altruistic social interest behaviors are associated with better mental health. Psychosomatic Medicine 2003;65:778-85.
[315] Lyubomirsky, S. The How of happiness. A New approach to getting the life you want. 2007. Penguin Books.
[316] Aspinwall LG, Brunhart SM. Distinguishing optimism from denial: optimistic beliefs predict attention to health threats. Personality and Social Psychology Bulletin 1996;22:993-1003.
[317] Segerstrom SC. Optimism, goal conflict, and stressor-related immune change. Journal of Behavioral Medicine 2001;24:437-59.
[318] Lyubomirsky, S. The How of happiness. A New approach to getting the life you want. 2007. Penguin Books.p.109.
[319] Sheldon KM, Lyubomirsky S. How to increase and sustain positive emotions: the effects of expressing gratitude and visualizing best possible selves. Journal of Positive Psychology 2006;1:73-82.
[320] Pennebaker JW, Graybeal A. patterns of natural language use: disclosure, personality, and social integration. Current Directions in Psychological Science 2001;10:90-3.
[321] Lyubomirsky, S. The How of happiness. A New approach to getting the life you want. 2007. Penguin Books.p.108.
[322] Havighurst RJ, Glasser R. An exploratory study of reminiscing. Psychology and Aging;2003;18:430-2.
[323] Lyubomirsky, S. The How of happiness. A New approach to getting the life you want. 2007. Penguin Books.p.200.
[324] Bryant F, Veroff J. Savoring: A new model of Positive Experience. 2006. Mahwah, NJ: Erlbaum.
[325] Lyubomirsky, S. The How of happiness. A New approach to getting the life you want. 2007. Penguin Books.p185.
[326] Thompson C. Meet the life hackers. New York Times, October 16, 2005, citing a study performed at UC-Irvine.
[327] Leyden J. One in five US firms has sacked workers for email abuse. In www.theregister.co.uk, on June 23, 2003.
[328] Seligman MEP, Steen TA, Park N, Peterson C. Positive psychological progress: empirical validation of interventions. American psychologist 2005;60:410-21.
[329] Saks AM. Longitudinal field investigation of the moderating and mediating effcts of self-efficacy on the relationship between training and newcomer adjustment. Journal of Applied Psychology 1995;80:211-25.
[330] Dillon S. Study sees an Obama effect as lifting black test-takers. New York Times, January 22, 2009.
[331] Blackwell LS, Trzesnieswki KH, Dweck CS. Implicit theories of intelligence predict achievement across adolescent transition: a longitudinal study and an intervention. Child Development 2007;78:246-63.
[332] Achor S. The happiness advantage. 2010. Crown business, Random House, New York.p.53.
[333] Keller MC, Fredrickson BL, et al. A warm heart and a clear head: the contingent effects of mood and weather on cognition. Psychological Science 2005;16:724-31.
[334] Babyak M, Blumenthal J, Herman S, et al. Exercise treatment for major depression: maintenance of therapeutic effect at 10 months. Psychological Medicine 2000;62:633-8.
[335] Lutz A, Greischar LL, Rawlings NB, Ricard M, Davidson RJ. Long-term meditators self-induce high-amplitude gamma synchrony during mental practice. Proc Natl Acad Sci U S A. 2004 Nov 16;101(46):16369-73.
[336] Shapiro SL, Scwartz GER, Santerre C. meditation and positive psychology. 2005. In Snyder CR, Lopez SJ. Handbook of positive psychology. Oxford University Press, New York. p.632-45.
[337] Just the expectation of a mirthful laughter experience boosts endorphins 27 percent. American Physiological Society, at wwww.physorg.com/news63293074.html.
[338] Lyubomirsky, S. The How of happiness. A New approach to getting the life you want. 2007. Penguin Books.
[339] Lyubomirsky S, Sheldon KM, Schkade D. Pursuing happiness: the architecture of sustainable change. Review of General Psychology. 2005;9:111-31.
[340] Maxwell Maltz. Psycho-cybernetics. 1979.
[341] Thaler RH, Sunstein C. Nudge: improving decisions about health, wealth, and happiness. 2008. Penguin, New York.
[342] Lyubomirsky, S., King, L., and Diener, E. The benefits of frequent positive affect: Does happiness lead to success? Psychological Bulletin. 2005;131:803.

Acknowledgments

Idahlynn Karre and Jason Baxter,
for their helpful review and edits